D1596081

Private Lending to Sovereign States

Private Lending to Sovereign States:
A Theoretical Autopsy

Daniel Cohen

The MIT Press
Cambridge, Massachusetts
London, England

This book was set in Palatino by Asco Trade Typesetting Ltd., Hong Kong and printed and bound in the United States of America.

Library of Congress Cataloging-in-Publication Data

Cohen, Daniel.
 Private lending to sovereign states: a theoretical autopsy / by Daniel Cohen.
   p. cm.
 Includes bibliographical references and index.
 ISBN 0-262-03172-8
 1. Debts, Public—Developing countries. 2. Loans, Foreign—Developing countries.
3. Debt relief—Developing countries. 4. Government spending policy—Developing
countries. I. Title.
HJ8899.C643   1991
336.3′435′091724—dc20
                                                                90-46185
                                                                CIP

To my parents.
To my brother.
To a rising star, David-Emmanuel C.
To my friends.
For Anne.

Contents

Acknowledgments

This work is a distant version of my "Thèse de Doctorat d'Etat," which I defended at the University of Paris-X in February 1986 and whose English version was circulated as a monograph entitled "Money, Wealth and the Debt of Nations." This revised version only deals with the last theme of the previous version. I should like to express my grateful appreciation to all my professors, colleagues, and friends, without whose assistance and support it could never have been completed. A special word of thanks must go to Professors Pierre Llau, Jean-Pascal Benassy, Pierre Cortesse, Claude Fourgeaud, Pierre-Yves Henin, and Françoise Renversez, to Jean-Michel Grandmont, who published the French version, and to Rudi Dornbusch, whose lectures I enjoyed (as he would say) so much attending. A large part of the work presented here was completed while I was a consultant at the World Bank. I am most thankful to Nick Hope, John Underwood, Homi Kharas, and to all the members of the External Debt Division for their very warm hospitality.

My deepest intellectual debt is undoubtedly to Jeffrey Sachs, who taught me how to use neoclassical economics, and to Suzanne de Brunhoff, who alerted me to its pitfalls.

Particular thanks, too, to Philippe Michel and Philippe Weil, with whom I have so enjoyed working; may we continue to work together in fruitful and friendly collaboration. I am most grateful, too, to Olivier Blanchard for making the round trip to Paris specially to be part of the thesis committee.

My heartfelt thanks to Christiane Pillard for her splendid typing. Only she knows the pains involved in writing—and rewriting—so many pages in two different languages. Many thanks too to Joyce Schonfield, who helped me translate the first version of this book.

This work is dedicated to the memory of Jean Ibanes, a dear friend, who introduced me to economics and whose death still darkens the lives of all who knew him.

Introduction

In the early 1970s, the total debt of developing countries was less than 100 billion dollars. By the end of the 1980s, it had passed the trillion-dollar mark. In the meantime, we have lost the illusion that the debt would be repaid in full. On the secondary market on which lenders sell their claims, large debtors such as Mexico, Brazil, and Argentina saw their discount rise above 50% (figure I.1 in the appendix). In some extreme cases, such as Sudan, the price of the debt reached a 95% discount.

How did it all happen? It is in the nature of the banking business to make risky loans, and it is in the nature of competition to price risk appropriately. In the case of the loans to less-developed countries (LDCs), however, there was hardly any risk premium asked at the time the loans were made. Lenders were sometimes quoted as saying that countries never go insolvent the way private firms do. It was in quasi-euphoria that the large liquidities in search of investments—produced by the OPEC surpluses—were channeled by private banks to the LDCs. It was seen as a triumph of the efficiency of capital markets that savings could so aptly be funneled to investments.

It takes one generation, it seems, to forget the lessons of history. History, indeed, is filled with episodes that contradict the 1970s dictum that countries do not go bankrupt. In the 1930s, widespread default accompanied the Great Depression. In the nineteenth century, default was a recurrent feature of sovereign debt. Earlier on, Philippe le Bel of France and Charles V of Spain, among many others, showed the way of default to later rulers.

Default on foreign debt should come as no surprise. Defaulting on external debt is indeed a typical tool of domestic sovereignty. A sovereign state has no law above its head that it must obey simply because the "law is the law." Honoring any international contract must be seen as a net benefit. In the case of a firm, instead, it is by simple virtue of their legal claim that banks or bondholders take over a defaulting firm. In the case of a sovereign debtor, it can only be the fear of (direct or indirect) sanctions that forces the debtor to honor its debt to foreign creditors.

The costs of default is a favorite topic of lawyers. Kaletsky (1985) reviews them at length. A defaulting country first loses access to its trade credit. Then its foreign assets may be seized. Trade, in general, becomes difficult, exporting is tricky, and so is paying for its imports. Domestic costs must be added. Financial instability triggers capital flight. All of these costs and others pile up. Before defaulting on its debt, a country must carefully balance the pluses and minuses of its decision.

However large the costs of default may be, they are not infinite. There will always be some level of debt at which a sovercign debtor will default rather than servicing it in full. This may happen even though the country has the resources needed to service the debt. There is little doubt indeed that Brazil's wealth far exceeds the 100-billion-dollar level that its debt passed in the mid-1980s. It is Brazil's political willingness to pay, rather than Brazil's strict capacity to pay, that is the core uncertainty inducing lenders to sell Brazil's debt below par.

If this is so, why is it that lenders did not seem to pay any attention to these consideration in the 1970s, when they made their loans? The reason, developed in chapter 2, is the following: in the 1970s, real interest rates were below the growth rates of the debtors' economies. This state of nature implies that time can solve any debt crisis: rescheduling the debt always reduces the debt-to-GDP or the debt-to-export ratio of a fast-growing economy. Postponing the service of the debt is therefore always feasible. Yet, as I emphasize, this idyllic state of affairs could not be expected to last forever. The probability of some change in the hierarchy between growth and interest rates had to be taken into account, by both lenders and borrowers. Otherwise, why did borrowers not borrow *more* if they knew that they could always postpone the burden of servicing the debt?

The oddity of the change of economic regime of the 1980s was not so much that it happened, but perhaps that it happened as a worldwide phenomenon. Lenders and borrowers may have taken into account the risk of a slowdown in countries' idiosyncratic growth patterns. However, a large rise in world interest rates above so many of these economies' growth rates may have come as a total surprise to any banker educated in the 1960s, when real interest rates were near zero while growth was averaging 5% worldwide.

Whatever its origin, however, it soon appeared that the economic environment of the 1980s completely changed the rules of the game inherited from the 1970s. Time was no longer on the debtor's side. Postponing the repayment of the debt would now trap the borrower through the law of compound interest. New loans rapidly dried up and borrowers were soon out of cash. In the infamous summer of 1982, Mexico suspended the payment of its debt and was soon followed by Brazil, Argentina, and a cohort of other highly indebted developing countries.

At that moment, lenders realized that Mexico's oil wealth was not collateral at all. The money they so carelessly lent, which they so desperately wanted to get back, depended on the Mexican government's *political willingness* to impose on its people and constituency the austerity measures needed to transfer abroad whatever income was required to service the debt.

This uncollateralized nature of sovereign debt is the key feature that this book intends to exploit. The specific nature of debt rescheduling, the game between small and large banks, the risk of a bank panic, the inefficiency of the credit market when lenders lack the capability of committing themselves to a lending policy—these are crucial features of the credit market to sovereign states, which appear to the direct consequences of the absence of collateral on which lenders can mortgage their loans.

In the summer of 1982, there was a basic uncertainty on the debtor's perceived balance of costs and benefits associated with debt service. Would Mexico, Brazil, Argentina, and the others find it in their interest to service the debt? Would the threats that the lenders could muster be sufficient to induce them to accept the International Monetary Fund's stabilization program? At that time, one could only try to guess the potential impact of each of the items Kaletsky would later review. No one—at the time—tried to undertake such a calculation. The uncertainties were enormous.

Less than two years later, however, many borrowers revealed that they were ready to go some way toward accepting the lenders' conditions. From 1982 to 1989, the fifteen most highly indebted nations managed to turn their trade balance deficits into substantial trade surpluses (see "Net transfers," tables I.1 and I.2, and figure I.3 in the appendix). With the insight of these later developments, can one *now* argue that Brazil or Mexico was "solvent" in December 1982, with "solvent" meaning that they would have preferred to service their debt rather than default? Part of this book is aimed at answering this question.

One of the key features of private lending to a sovereign debtor that sheds light on this question is as follows: On the one hand, a country's solvency certainly cannot be gauged by its ability to pay the interest or the principal falling due. Postponing the payment of part of the interest falling due amounts to letting the debt grow. To the extent that the country itself is growing, this need not be damaging, provided that (at least asymptotically) the debt is kept from growing more rapidly than the economy itself. In contrast to the case of a firm, however, the timing of payments is crucial. Postponing the payment of the interest due by a firm by one year should not harm the lenders very much if the firm invests those resources (raising the collateral the lenders can put their hands on later; this is essentially the Modigliani-Miller theorem). In the case of a country, one year's foregone payments may be lost forever by the lenders. This is indeed one implication of the constraint that the borrower has to be willing to service its debt out of its own consumption. Lenders cannot be tougher on a country one year because they were nicer the year before.

On the other hand, if a country has been *observed* to prefer giving up, say, 2% of its GDP rather than defaulting, one may have an indication that, ceteris paribus, it is a choice that the country will also be willing to make later on. Taking this result for granted (the conditions for which it holds are spelled out in chapter 5), one can calculate the minimum fraction of a country's resources that the country must have been *observed* to transfer abroad in order for the country to be declared solvent. These calculations are performed in chapter 6. I estimate that it takes 15% of a country's exports to protect the country's solvency. I compare this number to the actual transfers performed by debtors in the 1980s. This comparison shows that, among other countries, Brazil and Mexico successfully passed this test of solvency in the mid-1980s.

If this is so, what then went wrong in these two countries? If indeed Brazil and Mexico were solvent in December 1982, why is it that by the late 1980s their situation was considered so bad that their lenders were ready to exchange a claim of one dollar on Brazil or Mexico against less than 50 cents in cash?

As far as Brazil is concerned, I show in chapter 7 that the country itself may be solvent but its *government* is not. Brazil's government is shown to have been incapable of raising taxes or reducing expenditures, steps that were needed to service the country's debt. As a result, domestic debt went up as an (almost) exact counterpart of the service of the foreign debt and eventually crowded out the domestic financial markets to the point of asphyxiation. The policy implication is that Brazil should have been entitled to service a lesser portion of its debt against the promise of a domestic tax reform.

Mexico did not experience the same domestic difficulties. The sources of Mexico's problems are elsewhere and obvious: they hinge on the 1987 collapse in the price of oil. The enormous policy mistake made in the wake of the 1982 crisis was to fail to index the debt to the price of oil. The IMF did propose an indexation scheme, but by then it was too late.

Whatever the origin of the buildup of debt, it appears that most highly indebted countries seem to have passed, in the late 1980s, the point at which they would rather default than pay their debt in full. To avoid such defaults, banks have been led to reschedule the debt of many countries (see table I.3). At the same time, most debtors have cut their investment rates well below the levels reached a decade earlier. Can it be argued that the debt is in itself the chief reason for the crowding out of investment, and that shortsighted management of the debt has failed to exploit profitable investment opportunities in the debtor countries? This question is addressed in the last part of this book. We shall see that the rescheduling of the debt may indeed be to blame for partially crowding out investment in an unnecessarily restrictive way. I argue, however, that the largest share of the decline in investment is due less to the quantitative burden of servicing the debt than to the qualitative change of economic regime from the 1970s to the 1980s, which switched the hierarchy between growth and interest rates.

In a nutshell, my argument is as follows: In the 1980s, all LDCs had to bear the burden of the increased cost of capital. For many of them, however indebted they may have been, this has primarily meant returning to a state of quasi financial autarky, hence to a rate of investment nearer that of the 1960s than that of the 1970s. In table I.4, one sees that all regions except East Asia experienced a growth of investment in the 1980s that was lower than that of GDP. For all regions but Latin America, however, the share of investment as a percentage of GDP remained slightly above the level experienced in the mid-1960s.

For the highly indebted nations as a whole (many of them Latin American), the investment rate did fall below its pre-1970s benchmark, and for those countries an undue crowding out of investment by the service of the debt can be detected. I show that—for the rescheduling countries—one dollar paid to their creditors crowds out investment by forty cents. I interpret (in chapter 9) this crowding out of investment in light of the "debt overhang" literature, which portrays the burden of servicing the external debt as an inefficient tax on the domestic economy. I suggest how the debt rescheduling should be designed so as to crowd *in* investment. We shall see in particular that maintaining the *fiction* that a country is solvent is counterproductive to the lenders themselves. What is needed to efficiently collect the debt service are clear rules of the game that acknowledge the market price of the debt. The book ends with a proposal as to what these rules should be.

Appendix: Tables and Figures

Table I.1
Public and private long-term debt and financial flows in developing countries, 1982–1988
(U.S.$ billions)

Long-term debt and financial flows	1982	1983	1984	1985	1986	1987	1988[a]
Debt disbursed and outstanding	562.5	644.9	686.7	793.7	893.9	996.3	1020.0
Disbursements	116.9	97.2	91.6	89.3	87.7	86.7	88.0
(from private creditors)	84.6	65.0	58.9	57.8	50.8	48.5	50.0
Debt service	98.7	92.6	101.8	112.2	116.5	124.9	131.0
Principal repayments	49.7	45.4	48.6	56.4	61.5	70.9	72.0
Interest	48.9	47.3	53.2	55.8	54.9	54.0	59.0
Net flows	67.2	51.8	43.0	32.9	26.2	15.8	16.0
Net transfers	18.2	4.6	−10.2	−22.9	−28.7	−38.1	−43.0

a. Preliminary estimates.
Source: *World Debt Table* (1988).

Table I.2
Highly indebted countries and the world economy, 1980–1988

	1980	1981	1982	1983	1984	1985	1986	1987	1988[c]
Economic growth indicators									
					Percentage real change				
Industrial country output	1.3	2.0	-0.4	2.8	4.5	3.1	2.7	3.3	3.9
World trade[a]	1.3	2.4	-1.0	3.0	9.9	4.0	2.6	4.3	7.5
HIC GDP[b]	5.6	0.6	-0.4	-2.9	1.9	3.7	3.4	1.7	2.0
HIC investment[b]	9.4	0.4	-13.1	-21.0	-2.1	4.5	1.9	0.8	-2.9
HIC per capita consumption[b]	3.4	0.3	-2.2	-4.1	-1.7	0.2	2.6	-1.4	-0.6
HIC exports[b]	1.1	-6.6	0.0	5.0	9.3	2.2	0.7	0.4	6.4
HIC imports[b]	8.2	2.3	-14.1	-20.4	-1.1	-1.6	4.0	-1.7	2.0
					U.S.$ billions				
Total external debt	289.0	351.0	391.0	422.0	438.0	454.0	482.0	527.0	529.0
Net flows to HICs	28.6	43.7	34.6	19.1	13.3	6.0	4.5	6.2	7.6
Net resource transfers to HICs	8.8	18.3	3.7	-9.9	-19.9	-26.5	-25.8	-21.8	-31.1

a. Volume. b. Constant 1980 U.S. dollars. c. Preliminary estimates.
Source: *World Debt Table* (1988).

Table I.3
Rescheduling agreements

Country	Consolidation period		Country	Consolidation period	
	Beginning data	Length (months)		Beginning data	Length (months)
Argentina			**Congo, People's Republic of the**		
Commercial banks			Commercial banks		
Jan 83			Feb 88	Jan 86	36
Aug 83			Official creditors		
Aug 85	Jan 82	48	Jul 86	Aug 86	20
Aug 87			**Costa Rica**		
Official creditors			Commercial banks		
Jan 85	Jan 85	12	Sep 83	Jan 83	24
May 87	May 87	14	May 85	Jan 85	24
Bolivia			Official creditors		
Commercial banks			Jan 83	Jul 82	18
Dec 80	Aug 80	8	Apr 85	Jan 85	15
Apr 81	Apr 81	24	**Ivory Coast**		
May 83	Jan 83	36	Commercial banks		
Official creditors			May 85	Dec 83	25
Jul 86	Jul 86	12	Nov 86	Jan 86	48
Brazil			Apr 88	Jan 83	96
Commercial banks			Official creditors		
Feb 83	Jan 83	12	May 84	Dec 83	13
Jan 84	Jan 84	12	Jun 85	Jan 85	12
Sep 86	Jan 85	12	Jun 86	Jan 86	36
Sep 88	Jan 87	84	Dec 87	Jan 88	16
Official creditors			**Cuba**		
Nov 83	Aug 83	17	Commercial banks		
Jan 87	Jan 85	30	Dec 83	Sep 82	28
Jul 88	Aug 88	20	Dec 84	Jan 84	12
Central African Republic			Jul 85	Jan 85	12
Commercial banks			Official creditors		
Jun 81	Jan 81	12	Mar 83	Sep 82	16
Jul 83	Jan 83	12	Jul 84	Jan 84	12
Nov 85	Jul 85	18	Jul 85	Jun 85	12
Chile			Jul 86	Jan 86	12
Commercial banks			**Dominican Republic**		
Jul 83	Jan 83	24	Commercial banks		
Jan 84			Dec 83	Dec 82	13
Jun 84			Feb 86	Jan 85	60
Nov 84			Official creditors		
Nov 85	Jan 85	36	May 85	Jan 85	15
Jun 87	Jan 88	48	**Ecuador**		
Apr 88			Commercial banks		
Official creditors			Oct 83	Nov 82	14
Jul 85 +	Jul 85	18	Dec 85	Jan 85	60
Apr 87 +	Apr 87	21	Nov 87*		
Colombia			Official creditors		
Commercial banks			Jul 83	Jun 83	12
Dec 85			Apr 85	Jan 85	36
			Jan 88	Jan 88	14

Table I.3 (continued)

Country	Consolidation period Beginning data	Length (months)
Egypt		
Official creditors		
May 87	Jan 87	18
Equatorial Guinea		
Official creditors		
Jul 85	Jan 85	18
Gabon		
Commercial banks		
Dec 87	Sep 86	27
Official creditors		
Jan 87	Sep 86	15
Mar 88	Jan 88	12
Gambia		
Commercial banks		
Feb 88	Dec 86	
Official creditors		
Sep 86	Oct 86	12
Guinea		
Official creditors		
Apr 86	Jan 86	14
Guinea-Bissau		
Official creditors		
Oct 87	Jul 87	18
Guyana		
Commercial banks		
Aug 82	Mar 82	13
Mar 83	Apr 83	3
Jun 83	Jul 83	7
Jan 84	Jan 84	6
Jul 84	Aug 84	12
Jul 85	Aug 85	18
Honduras		
Commercial banks		
Feb 83*	Jan 83	24
Dec 84*	Jan 86	48
Jun 87*	Jan 87	36
Jamaica		
Commercial banks		
Apr 81	Apr 79	24
Jun 81	Jul 81	21
Jun 84	Jul 83	21
Sep 85	Apr 85	24
May 87	Apr 87	39

Country	Consolidation period Beginning data	Length (months)
Official creditors		
Jul 84	Jan 84	15
Jul 85	Apr 85	12
Mar 87	Jan 87	15
Liberia		
Commercial banks		
Dec 82	Jul 81	24
Official creditors		
Dec 80	Jul 80	18
Dec 81	Jan 82	18
Dec 83	Jul 83	12
Dec 84	Jul 84	12
Madagascar		
Commercial banks		
Nov 81		
Oct 84	Dec 82	
Official creditors		
Apr 81	Jan 81	18
Jul 82	Jul 82	12
Mar 84	Jul 83	18
May 85	Jan 85	15
Oct 86	Apr 86	21
Malawi		
Commercial banks		
Mar 83	Sep 82	24
Apr 88	Aug 87	
Official creditors		
Sep 82	Jul 82	12
Oct 83	Jul 83	12
Apr 88	Apr 88	14
Mauritania		
Official creditors		
Apr 85	Jan 85	15
May 86	Apr 86	12
Jun 87	Apr 87	14
Mexico		
Commercial banks		
Aug 83	Aug 82	26
Apr 84		
Mar 85	Jan 87	48
Aug 85	Jan 85	72
Oct 85		
Mar 87		
Aug 87	Jan 88	48
Official creditors		
Jun 83 +	Jul 83	6
Sep 86	Sep 86	18

Table I.3 (continued)

Country	Consolidation period Beginning data	Length (months)	Country	Consolidation period Beginning data	Length (months)
Morocco			**Peru**		
Commercial banks			Commercial banks		
Feb 86	Jan 83	24	Jan 80	Jan 80	12
Sep 87	Jan 85	48	Jul 83	Mar 83	12
Official creditors			Feb 84*	Mar 84	22
Oct 83	Sep 83	16	Official creditors		
Sep 85	Sep 85	18	Jul 83	May 83	12
Mar 87	Mar 87	16	Jun 84	May 84	15
Mozambique			**Philippines**		
Commercial banks			Commercial banks		
May 87*	May 87		Jan 86	Oct 83	38
Official creditors			Dec 87	Jan 87	72
Oct 84	Jul 84	12	Official creditors		
Jun 87	Jun 87	19	Dec 84	Jan 85	18
Nicaragua			Jan 87	Jan 87	18
Commercial banks			**Poland**		
Dec 80			Commercial banks		
Dec 81			Apr 82	Mar 81	9
Mar 82			Nov 82	Jan 82	12
Feb 84		12	Nov 83	Jan 83	12
Niger			Jul 84	Jan 84	48
Commercial banks			Sep 86	Jan 86	24
Mar 84	Oct 83	24	Aug 87*	Jan 88	72
Apr 86	Oct 85	39	Official sources		
Official creditors			Apr 81 +	May 81	8
Nov 83	Oct 83	12	Jul 85 +	Jan 82	36
Nov 84	Oct 84	14	Mar 86 +	Jan 86	12
Nov 85	Dec 85	12	Oct 87 +	Jan 88	12
Nov 86	Dec 86	12	**Romania**		
Apr 88	Dec 87	13	Commercial banks		
Nigeria			Dec 82	Jan 82	12
Official creditors			Jun 83	Jan 83	12
Jul 83			Sep 86	Jan 86	24
Sep 83			Sep 87*		
Nov 87	Apr 86	21	Official creditors		
Official creditors			Jul 82	Jan 82	12
Nov 86	Oct 86	15	May 83	Jan 83	12
Pakistan			**Senegal**		
Official creditors			Commercial banks		
Jan 81 +	Jan 81	18	Feb 84	May 81	38
Panama			May 85	Jul 84	24
Commercial banks			Official creditors		
Sep 83			Oct 81	Jul 81	12
Oct 85	Jan 85	24	Nov 82	Jul 82	12
Jan 87	Jan 87	12	Dec 83	Jul 83	12
Official creditors			Jan 85	Jan 85	18
Sep 85	Sep 85	16			

Table I.3 (continued)

Country	Consolidation period Beginning data	Length (months)
Nov 86	Jul 86	16
Nov 87	Nov 87	12
Sierra Leone		
Commercial banks		
Jan 84		
Official creditors		
Feb 80	Jul 79	30
Feb 84	Jan 84	12
Nov 86	Jul 86	16
Somalia		
Commercial banks		
Mar 85	Jan 85	12
Jul 87	Jan 87	24
Sudan		
Commercial banks		
Nov 81	Jan 80	
Mar 82		
Apr 83		
Apr 84		
Oct 85		
Official sources		
Mar 82	Jul 81	18
Feb 83	Jan 83	12
May 84	Jan 84	12
Tanzania		
Official creditors		
Sep 86	Oct 86	12
Togo		
Commercial banks		
Mar 80	Dec 82	
Oct 83	Dec 82	
Official creditors		
Feb 81	Jan 81	24
Apr 83	Jan 83	12
June 84	Jan 84	16
Jun 85	May 85	12
Mar 88	Jan 88	15
Turkey		
Commercial banks		
Mar 82		
Official creditors		
Jul 80+	Jul 80	36
Uganda		
Commercial banks		
Nov 81	Jul 81	12

Country	Consolidation period Beginning data	Length (months)
Official creditors		
Dec 82	Jul 82	12
Jun 87	Jul 87	12
Uruguay		
Commercial banks		
Jul 83	Jan 83	24
Jul 86	Jan 85	60
Nov 87	Jan 90	24
Venezuela		
Commercial banks		
Feb 86	Jan 83	72
Nov 87		
Yugoslavia		
Commercial banks		
Oct 83	Jan 83	12
May 84	Jan 84	24
Dec 85	Jan 85	48
Jul 88	Jan 88	24
Official Sources		
May 84+	Jan 84	12
May 85+	Jan 85	16
Apr 86+	May 86	23
Jul 88+	Apr 88	15
Zaire		
Commercial banks		
Apr 80	Dec 79	
Jan 83		12
Jun 84		12
May 85		12
May 86		12
May 87		12
Official creditors		
Jul 81	Jan 81	24
Dec 83	Jan 84	12
Sep 85	Jan 85	15
May 86	Apr 86	12
May 87	Apr 87	13
Zambia		
Commercial banks		
Dec 84*	Mar 83	34
Official creditors		
May 83	Jan 83	12
Jul 84	Jan 84	12
Mar 86	Jan 86	12

Source: *World Debt Tables* (1988).

Table I.4
LDCs' growth and investment

	Growth rate of GDP (%)		Growth rate of investment (%)		Level of investment % GDP	
	1965–1980	1980–1987	1965–1980	1980–1987	1965	1987
Sub-Saharan Africa	5.1	0.4	9.3	−8.3	14	16
East Asia	7.2	8.0	11.3	12.1	23	30
South Asia	3.8	4.8	4.6	3.7	18	22
Latin America and the Carribean	6.0	1.4	8.3	−4.5	20	18
All LDCs	5.9	4.0	8.6	3.0	21	24
Highly indebted countries	6.1	1.1	8.6	3.1	21	19

Source: *World Development Report* (1989).

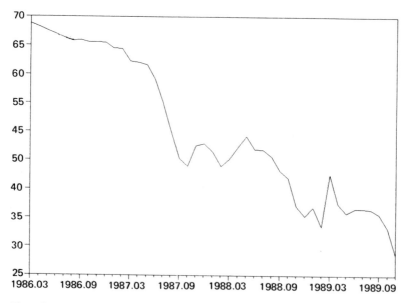

Figure I.1
Secondary market price of LDC debt (cents per dollar)

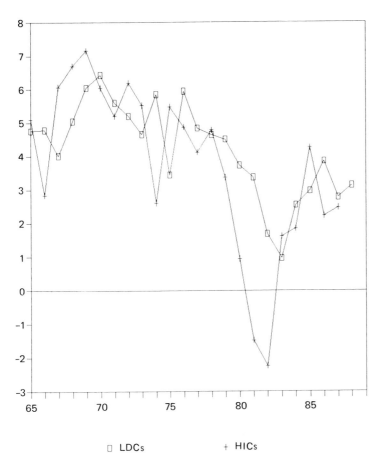

□ LDCs   + HICs

Figure I.2
GDP growth (constant prices)

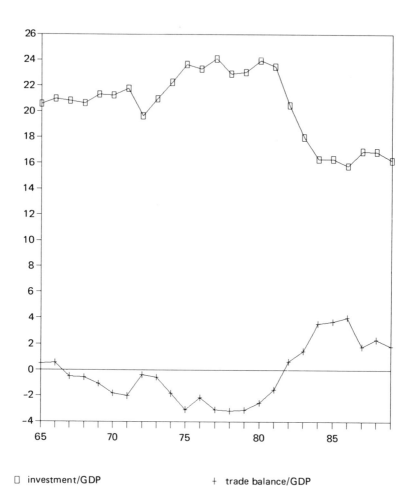

☐ investment/GDP   + trade balance/GDP

Figure I.3
Highly indebted countries' investment and trade balances (constant prices)

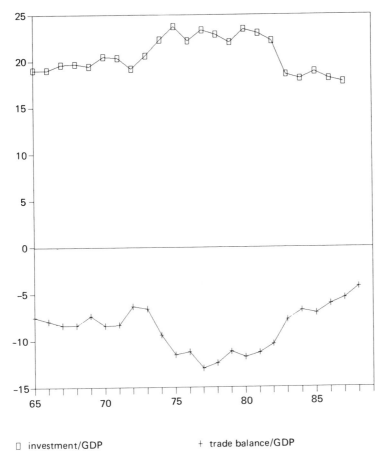

Figure I.4
Investment and trade balances of the high-debt developing countries (thirty-nine largest debtors, constant prices)

I BUDGET CONSTRAINTS FOR INDIVIDUALS AND FOR NATIONS

What was borrowed one day, another day should be repaid. For any individual, such a dictum is a fact of life. One may borrow when short of cash, when young, when facing advantageous investment opportunities. Whatever the reasons, the lenders will want to make sure that the debt will be repaid before the borrower dies. What is true for any individual agent should be true for any collection of agents facing the same time horizon. Take the baby-boom generation, composed of individuals born in the 1950s and most likely to be dead in the mid-twenty-first century. If a nation were solely inhabited by members of this generation, all debt accumulated by this nation (as a whole) vis-à-vis the rest of the world would certainly have to be repaid by the year 2050. This implies that the flows of net resources transferred to or from this nation by the rest of the world must "add up" to zero over the course of the nation's life (the summation must be appropriately measured in discounted terms). This result is essentially what chapter 1 spells out at some length.

What is true for an economy composed of only one generation of individuals does not necessarily hold true when the nation is composed of many overlapping generations of agents. While it must remain the case that the debt accumulated by any one generation cancels out over time, the financial flows between the nation as a whole and the rest of the world do not necessarily obey the same principles. It may appear that the debt borrowed by the new generations always exceeds the repayments made by older ones, so that the country as a whole will appear to be steadily borrowing new resources (in *net* terms) all the time. If every generation eventually pays off its debt, what's wrong with that? What's wrong is this: to the rest of the world as a whole, lending is an inefficient business. Indeed, a straightforward application of Samuelson's overlapping generations model shows that the rest of the world would be better off lending less and consuming more.

It does not take, as we shall see, a government of the rest of the world to monitor such a reduction in lending. It is enough that each government holds in check the balance of its own lending to the rest of the world. When this is done appropriately, a nation cannot find itself borrowing indefinitely. On average the debt of a nation (and not only the debt of each of its individuals) must be repaid.

The core of this analysis, it appears, hinges on the comparison between the growth rate of the economy and the rate of interest on world financial markets. The sign of an inefficient credit market equilibrium, as shown by

Samuelson (1958) and generalized by Cass (1972), is when interest rates are systematically below the growth rate of an economy. It is under these circumstances that a nation may find itself borrowing indefinitely from the rest of the world. Any casual observation of the thirty years spanning from the 1950s to the early 1980s shows that such a hierarchy between interest and growth rates has in fact prevailed. There was certainly no reason to expect in the 1970s that the hierarchy between the two rates would be reversed as early as the 1980s. I argue, however, that there must have been, at least implicitly, *some* assumption about a possible switch in the hierarchy between the two rates, not necessarily for the world as a whole but at least for each individual country. The surprise was that—all of a sudden—the switch caught *all* debtors in the trap of having to finance high interest rate payments out of slow growth.

1 Intertemporal Budget Constraints

In this introductory chapter I spell out the budget constraint to which each individual, government, and nation must be subject. For a finitely lived agent (household or institution), this budget constraint will always take a simple form: the present discounted value of what is spent is necessarily less than or equal to the present discounted value of what is earned. In this chapter these principles are aggregated for the nation as a whole in the case in which all individuals' economic horizons (however heterogeneous they may be) are encompassed by a common finite time horizon.

1.1 Households

Let us take a household i existing at some time $t \in \{0, \ldots, T\}$. The household agent owns financial wealth W_{t-1}^i, which he may have saved from previous times or inherited from his parents. We assume that there are no domestic or external debts at the initial time.

Let us call r_t the (given) world rate of interest that is imposed on the domestic economy at time t. The agent's wealth follows the law of motion:

$$W_t^i = (1 + r_t)W_{t-1}^i - C_t^i + y_t^i, \tag{1}$$

in which C_t^i is the agent's expenditures at time t and y_t^i is the net income paid to the agent for the work that he produced at time t.

If the agent dies at the end of time t, he may leave some bequest $W_t^i \geqslant 0$ to his children. He may also leave some debt—if the children love their parents enough to accept this financial burden. I will call α_t^i ($\leqslant 0$) the constraint that may be imposed on agent i's wealth because of an intergenerational constraint. Agent i's wealth is therefore imposed to satisfy

$$W_t^i \geqslant \alpha_t^i. \tag{2}$$

If $\alpha_{t_i}^i = 0$ when t_i is the time of agent i's death, this will imply that the bequest must be non-negative. Call $J_t^i(W_{t-1}^i)$ the utility that agent i expects at least to derive from his accumulated wealth W_{t-1}^i; let β be the agent's subjective discount factor and $u(C_t^i)$ the utility he derives from consuming C_t at time t. Agents i's problem may be formally written as

Maximize $\{u^i(C_t^i) + \beta J_{t+1}^i(W_t^i)\}$ subject to (1) and (2).
$\quad C_t^i$

We call $J_t^i(W_{t-1}^i)$ the left-hand side of this program:

$$J_t^i(W_{t-1}^i) \equiv \text{Max } \{u(C_t^i) + \beta J_{t+1}^i(W_t^i)\} \text{ subject to (1) and (2).} \tag{3}$$

If the agent dies at the end of time t, $J_{t+1}^i(W_t^i)$ represents the value of a bequest to his children or, if he does not die, $J_{t+1}^i(W_t^i)$ is the solution to a similar equation written at time $t + 1$. Because of our assumption that all agents (and their children) must die before T, the value $J^i(W)$ is unambiguously defined by backward induction.

For any agent born at time t_0 and about to die at time $t_0 + L$, the stream of spending $(C_t^i)_{t=t_0, \ldots, t_0+L}$ and the stream of earnings $(y_t^i)_{t=t_0, \ldots, t_0+L}$ associated with an accumulation or decumulation of the agent's wealth may be written as

$$\sum_{s=t_0}^{t_0+L} \frac{C_s^i}{\prod\limits_{u=t_0}^{s} (1 + r_u)} = \sum_{s=t_0}^{t_0+L} \frac{y_s^i}{\prod\limits_{u=t_0}^{s} (1 + r_u)} + W_{t_0-1}^i - \frac{W_{t_0+L}^i}{\prod\limits_{u=t_0}^{t_0+L} (1 + r_u)}. \tag{4}$$

This equation is a direct application of the "principles of actualization," which are spelled out in the appendix.

At the end of all time T, no agent will ever want to let any of his wealth go unspent (he will have no children to whom to leave any bequest), nor, for symmetric reasons, will he ever be entitled to borrow. It must therefore be that, for all agents i

$$W_T^i = 0, \quad \forall i. \tag{5}$$

Taking account of this terminal wealth constraint, aggregating over all agents i (with the notation that $C_t = \sum_i C_t^i$) and over all time horizons, equation (4) must necessarily yield the following equality:

$$\sum_{t=0}^{T} \frac{C_t}{\prod\limits_{i=0}^{t} (1 + r_i)} = W_{-1} + \sum_{t=0}^{T} \frac{y_t}{\prod\limits_{i=0}^{t} (1 + r_i)}. \tag{6}$$

The private agents will necessarily spend (when everything is appropriately measured in discounted terms) all of their initial financial wealth and all of their human wealth—no more, no less. This is a property that is independent of the constraint α_t^i imposed on bequests.

1.2   Firms

Firms are where production takes place. For simplicity, we shall assume that there is one representative firm in the economy. Production is defined through a production function:

$$Q_t = f(K_t, N_t), \tag{7}$$

in which N_t is labor hired by the firm at time t and K_t is the capital that is installed at that time. The law of motion of capital will be assumed to take the form

$$K_{t+1} = g(K_t, J_t). \tag{8}$$

It is a function of previous capital stock and of the investment decision J_t of the firm. A standard neoclassical model is $K_{t+1} = K_d(1 - d) + J_t$, in which d is the depreciation rate of the stock of capital. I also analyze (in chapters 8 and 9) a more sophisticated model in which installation costs may prevail.

Call X_t the profit kept by the firm. X_t is the after-tax, after-net-wage income of the firm, and T_t is taxes paid to the government:

$$X_t = Q_t - T_t - y_t.$$

From one period to another, the firm may contract financial obligation F_t with respect to outside suppliers of funds. The law of motion of the firm's cash flows is

$$X_t + F_t = (1 + r_t)F_{t-1} + DIV_t + J_t. \tag{9}$$

The left-hand side measures the resources that the firm has access to (profits and outside funds). The right-hand side spells out how these resources are allocated: they pay the interest and the principal on previous financial commitments; they pay dividends (DIV_t) to the shareholders; and the rest, J_t, is how much capital investment is undertaken.

Just like any individual, a firm may have a shorter life than T, the overall horizon of the economy. At any rate, if a firm dies at T, it must have repaid by then its financial commitments. (In the deterministic setting that we analyze, lenders know ahead of time when the firm will disappear.)

The stock value of the firm, V_t, is the sum of the dividends it pays at time t and the present discounted value at which the firm can be sold at time $t + 1$.

$$V_t = DIV_t + \frac{1}{1 + r_{t+1}} V_{t+1}.$$

If the firm's time horizon is the time interval (t_0, t_f), one sees that $V_{t_f} = 0$ (and perhaps $V_{t_0} = 0$ if the firm is in a competitive environment). At any rate, one can always write, at the initial time, the value of the firm as

$$V_{-1} = \sum_{0}^{T} \frac{DIV_t}{\prod\limits_{s=0}^{t} (1 + r_s)}.$$

Making use of equation (8) and taking account of the fact that the firm has zero initial debt and zero terminal wealth, this equation can be re-written as

$$V_{-1}' = \sum_{0}^{T} \frac{Q_t - J_t - T_t - y_t}{\prod\limits_{s=0}^{t} (1 + r_s)}.$$

This is a very simple version of the Modigliani-Miller theorem. It states that the value of the firm is the present discounted value of the firm's cash flows and does not depend on specific patterns of dividends generated by the firm.

1.3   Government

The government is assumed to live the whole T period. We shall assume that a government in office at time t accepts and does not repudiate the financial commitments inherited from previous governments. I assume that the government, like the private agents, has no outstanding debt at the beginning of time $t = 0$.

Call B_t the public debt of the government at a later time $t > 0$. Its law of motion can be written as

$$B_t = (1 + r_t)B_{t-1} + G_t - T_t, \tag{10}$$

in which G_t is a measure of government expenditures and T_t is government's taxation. Just like that of any other agent, a government's debt must obey $B_T = 0$.

At any time t, when a debt B_t has been accumulated, one can therefore write

$$B_t + \sum_{s=t+1}^{T} \frac{G_s}{\prod\limits_{u=t+1}^{s} (1 + r_u)} = \sum_{s=t+1}^{T} \frac{T_s}{\prod\limits_{u=t+1}^{s} (1 + r_u)}. \tag{11}$$

The left-hand side measures the burden of the debt and that of future expenditures. The right-hand side measures the resources that the government has access to through tax collection. Like any individual, a government must obey an intertemporal budget constraint that forces expenditures (the left-hand side) to equal income (the right-hand side). Taking account of the fact that $B_{-1} = 0$, (12) can be written

$$\sum_{t=0}^{T} \frac{G_t}{\prod_{s=0}^{t}(1+r_s)} = \sum_{t=0}^{T} \frac{T_t}{\prod_{s=0}^{t}(1+r_s)}. \tag{12}$$

We shall refer to this equation as the government's intertemporal budget constraint.

1.4   The Rest of the World

At any time t, the nation as a whole has produced Q_t invested J_t, and consumed C_t and G_t. Let us define total absorption as the nation's aggregate spending:

$$A_t = C_t + G_t + J_t. \tag{13}$$

The difference between the country's output, Q_t, and the country's absorption, A_t, is exported abroad if positive or imported from abroad if negative. The trade balance of the nation is defined as this difference between the country's resources at time t and the its aggregate spending at time t:

$$TB_t = Q_t - A_t, \tag{14}$$

We now want to show the simple but fundamental equality:

$$\sum_{t=0}^{T} \frac{TB_t}{\prod_{s=0}^{t}(1+r_u)} = 0. \tag{15}$$

The present discounted value of the country's trade flows with the rest of the world necessarily adds up to zero. This equality is nothing but the aggregation of the budget constraints of households, firms, and the government.

Consider equation (6). It states that the present discounted value of private agents' consumption is equal to their initial financial and human wealth. But their initial financial wealth must correspond to the firms' market value (indeed, we assumed that, at time $t = 0$, there is no inherited public debt nor any external financial commitment). It must therefore be the case that

$$W_{-1} = \sum_{t=0}^{T} \frac{Q_t - J_t - y_t - T_t}{\prod_{s=0}^{t}(1 + r_s)}. \tag{16}$$

From equation (16), one sees that

$$\sum_{0}^{T} \frac{C_t}{\prod_{s=0}^{t}(1 + r_s)} = \sum_{0}^{T} \frac{Q_t - J_t - T_t}{\prod_{s=0}^{t}(1 + r_s)}.$$

Making use of the government's budget constraint (12), it then follows straightforwardly that (15) must necessarily hold.

Equation (15) simply states that a nation obeys a budget constraint that mirrors the budget constraint obeyed by each of its members. No one, in this economy, should care specifically about the nation's budget constraint. It will necessarily be obeyed by virtue of aggregating each of its members' own budget constraints.

Appendix: Financial Markets and the Principle of Actualization

In this appendix, I spell out a basic equation that will be used repeatedly in this book. Let us consider a stock variable W_t, which is related to a flow variable X_t according to the following law of motion:

$$W_t = (1 + r_t)W_{t-1} - X_t. \tag{A1}$$

A typical example is when W_{t-1} measures the outstanding wealth that an agent holds at the end of time $t - 1$; $r_t W_{t-1}$ is the interest (or dividends) accruing to him during time t; X_t is how much this agent spends during that time. Other instances (such as the pricing of a security) will also be shown to obey an equation such as (A1).

Let us now consider an interval of time $[t, t + h]$ over which the law of motion (1) is valid. During the $h + 1$ periods that are covered by this interval, let us assume that we know perfectly the original value W_{t-1} and each of the $h + 1$ flow variables $X_t, \ldots, X_{t+h}$ that are forthcoming. How can one simply relate the terminal value W_{t+h} to its original value W_{t-1} and to the sequence $(X_t, \ldots, X_{t+h})$? A simple technique is as follows. Write equation (A1) at any time $t + i$ as

$$\frac{W_{t+i}}{\prod\limits_{s=t}^{t+i}(1 + r_s)} = \frac{W_{t+i-1}}{\prod\limits_{s=t}^{t+i-1}(1 + r_s)} - \frac{X_{t+i}}{\prod\limits_{s=t}^{t+i}(1 + r_s)}. \tag{A2}$$

Equation (A2) is equation (A1) predivided on both sides by $\prod_{s=t}^{t+i}(1 + r_s)$, the compound interest between t and $t + i$. By adding all such equations (A2) obtained when i is varied between 0 and h, one finds

$$\frac{W_{t+h}}{\prod\limits_{s=t}^{t+h}(1 + r_s)} = W_{t-1} - \sum_{i=0}^{h}\frac{X_{t+i}}{\prod\limits_{s=t}^{t+i}(1 + r_s)}, \tag{A3}$$

which is a key equation that we shall term "the principle of actualization."

In the case in which W_t is the wealth of an agent and X_t is how much the agent spends at time t, equation (A3) simply indicates that the value of his wealth, h periods later, is equal to the value of the wealth he inherited from time $t - 1$ *minus* the present discounted value of all the spending he undertook between time t and time $t + h$.

2 Can a Nation Escape Its Budget Constraint?

In the previous chapter I demonstrated—in the context of a finitely lived economy—that it was enough that each member of a nation obeys its intertemporal budget constraint to ensure that the nation respects its own intertemporal budget constraint.

This chapter investigates whether this result can be extended to the case of an economy inhabited by an infinite number of overlapping generations of finitely lived agents. Relying on Samuelson 1958, we shall see that the budget constraint that holds true for each member of a nation does not necessarily hold true for the nation as a whole when the nation's growth rate exceeds the world interest rate. In particular, under such a hierarchy of growth and interest rates, a nation may very well be draining new resources all the time, even though each of its members repays his debts. This happy state of affairs (from the borrowing nation's viewpoint) may be a reminder of the 1970s, when fast growth and low interest rates may have let the debtor nations believe that they could keep borrowing endlessly. We shall see, however, that, this situation could not have been expected to continue with 100% probability. In other words, no nation can expect to escape its budget constraint forever. We shall then examine a "pseudo-Samuelsonian" economy, in which a nation can expect with a probability lower than one to avoid the burden of servicing its debt.

2.1 An Overlapping Generations Model

Consider an economy inhabited, at each point in time, by two categories of agents: young ones, born at time t, and old ones, born at time $t - 1$. Each generation only lives two periods, so that, at time $t + 1$, those born at time t will have become the old of time $t + 1$, and a new generation (at $t + 1$) will have appeared in the meantime; those born at time $t - 1$ are dead by time $t + 1$. No altruistic link will ever associate one generation with another. Each agent will individualistically maximize his own utility over the two periods of his life, with no respect to the newly born or the old generations.

With respect to the formulation written in equation (3) in the previous chapter, this amounts to assuming that an agent born at time t regards $J_{t+1}^i(W_t)$ as $u(W_t)$, or more simply, that any agent born at time t maximizes:

$$U[C_t(t), C_t(t + 1)] = u[C_t(t)] + \beta u[C_t(t + 1)]. \qquad (1)$$

Since no bequest is received from one's parents, one's only wealth is human wealth. I will only consider the simple case when it amounts to an endowment (ω_1, ω_2) at periods t and $t + 1$ respectively, which I assume is identical for each member of any generation.

On the other hand, generations are growing at a rate n, which is also a constant. Call N_t the number of young people alive at time t. The aggregate population alive is $N_t + N_{t-1} (= N_{t-1}[1 + 1/(1 + n)])$ and, for each period, the flow of resources available in the country is

$$Q_t = N_t \omega_1 + N_{t-1} \omega_2 = N_t \left(\omega_1 + \frac{1}{1 + n} \omega_2 \right). \tag{2}$$

Call y a representative member of the young generation and o a representative member of the old generation. Call r_{t+1} the interest rate that prevails on the world financial markets at time t. Each agent faces a budget constraint that can be written

$$C_t(t) + \frac{1}{1 + r_{t+1}} C_t(t + 1) \leqslant \omega_1 + \frac{1}{1 + r_{t+1}} \omega_2. \tag{3}$$

I will limit the analysis to the case when current and future consumption goods are gross substitutes, so that:

$$\frac{\partial C_t(t)}{\partial r_{t+1}} \leqslant 0. \tag{4}$$

Let us now investigate which equilibria can be obtained in such an economy.

2.2   Patterns of the Trade Balance

First consider the case in which the world rate of interest is a constant, r. We shall distinguish two cases, according to whether r is larger or smaller than the growth rate, n, of the domestic economy.

2.2.1   When Interest Rates Exceed Growth Rates

Begin by analyzing the case when $r > n$. Each agent born at time t must select a consumption path $[C_t(t), C_t(t + 1)]$ that maximizes his utility (1) along a budget constraint:

$$C_t(t) + \frac{1}{1+r} C_t(t+1) = \omega_1 + \frac{1}{1+r} \omega_2. \tag{5}$$

Call $S_t(t)$ this individual's saving at time t and $S_t(t+1)$ the corresponding saving at time $t+1$. One way to write the budget constraint of the individual is

$$S_t(t) + \frac{1}{1+r} S_t(t+1) = 0. \tag{6}$$

If the agent saves a positive amount at time t, he will dissave at time $t+1$ a corresponding amount inflated by the interest rate. (The converse will be true if the agent is a borrower when young.) Because of the stationary nature of the problem—one can simply call S_y the saving of any young agent and S_0 the saving of any old agent—we may write (6) as

$$S_y + \frac{1}{1+r} S_o = 0. \tag{7}$$

Now consider the trade balance of the economy at any time t. Let us first consider the initial $t = 0$ when the economy is open—for the first time—to the world financial markets. At that time $t = 0$, only the young individuals are active in these markets. Indeed, no old agent will be able to borrow (he will be dead by the time $t = 1$ when the lenders will ask for repayment), nor will he be willing to lend (for the obvious opposite reason). The trade balance of the country at this initial time will be characterized as

$$TB_0 = N_0 S_y, \tag{8}$$

in which N_0 is the number of young alive at time $t = 0$.

At any later time $t > 0$, the trade balance will be a result of the young's initial decision to lend or to borrow *and* a result of the old's savings or dissavings. We can write the trade balance as

$$TB_t = N_t S_y + N_{t-1} S_o. \tag{9}$$

Taking account of the intertemporal budget constraint (6), this yields

$$TB_t = N_t S_y \left[1 - \frac{1+r}{1+n} \right],$$

that is,

$$TB_t = -N_t S_y \left[\frac{r-n}{1+n} \right] \tag{10}$$

In the case in which $r > n$, at any time $t > 0$ the trade balance will have an opposite sign to the initial trade balance attained when $t = 0$. In the case in which the opening to the world financial markets induces the young generation, say, to borrow, the country *as a whole* will in fact only borrow in net terms during the lifetime of this very first generation. Forever after, the flow of repayments by the old generations will always exceed the flow of new money that is drained into the country by the (new) young generations. This is simply because the law of coumpound interest tilts the balance of resources in favor of repayments.

It is straightforward to check, in that case, that the present discounted values of all the forthcoming trade flows add up to zero, that is, that

$$\sum_0^\infty \frac{TB_t}{(1+r)^t} = 0. \tag{11}$$

Indeed

$$TB_t = -SN_0 \frac{r-n}{1+n}(1+n)^t; \quad t > 0$$

$$TB_0 = S_y, \quad t = 0.$$

So checking that equation (11) holds true simply amounts to checking that

$$S_y = S_y \sum_1^\infty \frac{r-n}{1+n}\left(\frac{1+n}{1+r}\right)^t,$$

which is indeed always satisfied. We see, therefore, that the basic relationship that applied in the finitely lived economy is extended to the case of an infinitely lived economy.

2.2.2 When Interest Rates Are below the Growth Rate of the Economy

Let us now consider the case in which $r \leqslant n$. Formally, the same equation as (10) holds when the world interest rate is lower than the growth rate of the economy. Unlike in the previous case, a country that is initially a debtor will keep borrowing forever (or at least, when $r = n$, it will never repay its debt). It is important to emphasize that each generation does pay its debt. In the aggregate, however, the new debt borrowed from abroad always exceeds the repayments made by the previous generation. Conversely, if the country was originally a lender, it would keep lending to the rest of the world forever once it started to acquire assets on the world financial markets.

A simple application of the Samuelson's (1958) overlapping generations model demonstrates that, under these circumstances, the equilibrium is inefficient for the rest of the world when the country is a debtor, and inefficient for the country itself when it is a lender.

a) The Lender's View   Let us start with this latter case and assume that the country is originally a lender. At the world rate of interest, the young generations lend to the rest of the world and consume the proceeds of their savings when old. To understand why such lending activity is inefficient, consider what would happen if the government were to ban all lending to the world financial markets. Given the hypothesis in equation (4), it is clear that the domestic interest rate would have to fall to bring the young generation's savings rate down to zero. (The members of the young generation cannot lend to the old generation so that, at financial autarky, the young generation cannot save at all.) This move certainly works against the welfare of the young. Let us now assume that the government issues a domestic debt sufficient to bring the interest rate back to the world level. The situation of the young generation is now the same as before, if they can only make sure that they will not be taxed, when old, to finance the government's debt. To the extent that the interest rate is smaller than the growth rate of the economy, it is easy to see why they do not run such a risk. I now show that the government can indeed raise the same level of debt in the future (from the new young generations) in order to finance the repayments due to the bondholders. Indeed, call B_0 the debt the government can initially borrow so as to bring the domestic interest rate to the world financial markets. One has

$$B_0 = N_0 S_y,$$

which is the amount of savings that the young generations would have generated had they access to the world financial markets. At time 1, the government owes $B_0(1 + r)$. At the same rate of interest, r, the savings of the young generation (at time 1) are

$$S_1(1) = N_1 S_y = (1 + n)N_0 S_y = (1 + n)B_0,$$

which is larger than B_1 because $n > r$. The government can therefore easily finance the debt B_1 falling due and, in addition, distribute the difference B_0 $(n - r)$ to whomever it wants. Obviously, the same operation can be indefinitely repeated.

As a result, the government can simply mimic the world rate of interest and avoid the net transfer of wealth to the rest of the world that would result from the laissez-faire equilibrium: it necessarily Pareto-improves the welfare of the nation.

b) The Collective Rationality of Lenders   Let us now consider the case when the country is a debtor. By using exactly the same argument as in the previous case, one sees that the rest of the world, as a whole would lose from the participation of the debtor in the world financial markets. If the rest of the world consisted of only one country, it could simply ban foreign lending and make sure of raising its domestic welfare by issuing a domestic debt.

What would happen in the case in which the lenders consist of N separate countries? If they could coordinate their actions, they could certainly mimic what one country alone could do and distribute among themselves the benefit of keeping the debtor from joining the world financial markets.

What would happen if they could *not* coordinate their actions, say, because they do not speak the same language? There are many ways to answer this question, but one of the most interesting is to follow an approach developed in Tirole 1982. For the N governments of these N countries, lending to the rest of the world is a collectively inefficient process. Can they *each* anticipate that the *other* countries will bear the burden of the inefficiency? Tirole has shown that this is impossible. When an equilibrium is inefficient for a finite number of players, at least one of them realize that the equilibrium penalizes him or her. In our framework, this implies that at least one lending country would be better off by withdrawing from the world financial markets rather than maintaining the laissez-faire equilibrium.

If the $N - 1$ remaining countries still find themselves in a socially inefficient situation, one after another will withdraw from the financial markets until—eventually—aggregate lending becomes efficient.

To conclude, we see from this section that we can rule out the case in which world interest rates are below any debtor growth rate. A borrowing country cannot keep draining resources from abroad without necessarily reducing the welfare of at least one lender.

2.3 Economies with Finite Wealth

2.3.1 The Wealth of a Nation

Let us define the wealth of a nation as the present discounted value of the nation's income. If Q_t is the country's GDP at time t, the wealth of the nation is

$$W = \sum_{t=0}^{\infty} \frac{Q_t}{\prod_{s=0}^{t} (1 + r_s)}. \tag{12}$$

In the case of the overlapping generations economy, which we analyzed in the previous section, W could be simply defined as

$$W = \sum_{0}^{\infty} \frac{1}{(1 + r)^t} N_t \left[\omega_1 + \frac{1}{1 + n} \omega_2 \right] \tag{13}$$

In the case in which $n \leq r$, the wealth of the nation—so defined—is infinite. In contrast, when $r > n$, the right-hand side of equation (13) converges toward a finite number.

In the case of a small, open economy, we were able to rule out the case in which $r \leq n$. In such a case, the lending countries would gain by barring the debtors from their domestic financial markets. (Such an instance may be reminiscent of the U.S. interest equalization tax in the 1960s.) It is interesting to note that the finiteness of wealth rules out the case $r = n$, which can be shown (see Samuelson 1958 or Cass 1972) to be Pareto-efficient. Indeed, as we have shown, the case $r = n$ corresponds to an equilibrium that is Pareto-inefficient for the lenders but not necessarily for the world as a whole.

There is another (and more direct) way to rule out the case in which the wealth of the nation is infinite. Assume that the government can tax a fraction ε, however small it may be, of the private sector's wealth. When the wealth of the nation is W, the government's resources are εW. If the wealth of the nation were infinite *and* if the governments of the world

behaved noncooperatively on the world financial markets, the governmet
would face no budget restraint and each of them would certainly like to
consume indefinitely. For any of these two reasons, we shall consequently
assume that the equilibrium wealth of the nation has to be finite.

2.3.2   The Budget Constraint of a Nation with Finite Wealth

If we restrict our analysis to the case of a nation whose wealth is finite, it
now becomes a straightforward exercise to check that the nation obeys an
intertemporal budget constraint. To simplify the presentation, let us aggregate as a single individual a chain of generations for which the bequest
motive operates. Call i any such individual and let Q^i represent the income
to which this individual is entitled, and let A^i be his spending. Let (t_i, T_i)
be the time horizon of this individual. Any such agent must obey his own
intertemporal budget constraint:

$$\sum_{t_i}^{T_i} \frac{A_t^i}{\prod\limits_{s=t_i}^{t}(1+r_s)} = \sum_{t_i}^{T_i} \frac{Q_t^i}{\prod\limits_{s=t_i}^{t}(1+r_s)}.$$

Aggregating these equalities over all individuals yields

$$\sum_{0}^{\infty} \frac{A_t}{\prod\limits_{s=0}^{t}(1+r_s)} = \sum_{0}^{\infty} \frac{Q_t}{\prod\limits_{s=0}^{t}(1+r_s)}, \tag{14}$$

in which $A_t = C_t + G_t + J_t$ is aggregate spending and Q_t is GDP. This
equality does not depend upon the fact that the wealth is finite; it simply
aggregates all agent's budget constraints and is necessarily always satisfied.
What now depends crucially upon the fact that the wealth of the nation is
finite is the equivalence between equation (14) and the following:

$$\sum_{t=0}^{\infty} \frac{TB_t}{\prod\limits_{s=0}^{t}(1+r_s)} = 0. \tag{15}$$

Indeed, if both sides of equation (14) are finite, their difference must be zero
(remembering that $TB_t = Q_t - A_t$). This was not the case (as we have shown
when $r \leqslant n$) when each side of the equation was infinite.

Equation (15) is nothing but the generalization to the infinite horizon of
the intertemporal budget constraint that held true in the finite horizon case.
Just as in that case, finitely wealthy nations necessarily obey an inter-

temporal budget constraint, which is simply the result of each of the nation's member's own budget constraint.

2.3.3 The Current Account and the "Transversality Condition"

Let us spell out in more detail the implication of this equality for the current account of the country. Call D_t the net debt accumulated by the country at point t. D_t encapsules all financial flows between a nation and the rest of the world. D_t may be the result of firms', households', or governments' external borrowing. The law of motion of D_t is

$$D_t - D_{t-1} = r_t D_{t-1} - TB_t. \tag{16}$$

Indeed, in net terms, the debt may increase because of additional trade balance desequilibria or because of the flows of interest (rD_{t-1}) falling due. $TB_t - rD_{t-1}$ is the *current account* of the country; it measures the net flows of goods and financial services between the country and the rest of the world.

Starting with an initial debt $D_{-1} = 0$ (and using the principles of actualization outlined in the appendix to chapter 1), one can also write

$$\frac{D_t}{\prod_{s=0}^{t}(1 + r_s)} = \sum_{0}^{t} \frac{TB_t}{\prod_{s=0}^{t}(1 + r_s)}. \tag{17}$$

Equation (15) is therefore equivalent to

$$\lim_{t \to \infty} \frac{D_t}{\prod_{s=0}^{t}(1 + r_s)} = 0. \tag{18}$$

This equation is called the *transversality condition*. It states that the present discounted value of a nation's debt must tend toward zero in the long run, when (and only when) the nation is subject to the intertemporal budget constraint. (The terminology is borrowed from control theory; see Michel 1982).

It is crucial to note that that this condition does not imply that the debt itself should tend toward zero, or even toward a constant. It can very well be that the debt is growing at a rate $n > 0$ in the long run. The only constraint that this situation imposes on the debt is that $n < r$ if the interest rate r_t is a constant r. [The numerator in equation (18) must grow strictly less rapidly than the denominator.]

This transversality condition provides another way of checking the equivalence between the finiteness of the wealth and the intertemporal budget constraint (15) that the country as a whole must obey. Indeed, in an economy that is growing less rapidly than the world interest rate, each agent's budget constraint must certainly imply that the nation's debt (if it has any) grows less rapidly than the nation's income. Condition (18), hence condition (15), must therefore necessarily be satisfied.

2.4   A "Pseudo-Samuelsonian" Economy

According tᴗ the implications of the above model, world interest rates cannot *always* be below the growth rate of a debtor's economy. Now, it will appear that this state of affairs is not very far from that with which many borrowers in the 1970s thought they could live. Interest rates have indeed always been lower than growth rates in the thirty years from 1950 to 1980. The episodes during which interest rates were above growth rates in the twentieth century have been rare: they cover the years of the Great Depression in the 1930s, when price deflation and recession combined their effects to switch the hierarchy between rates. These episodes now include the 1980s. There is little doubt that the Reagan years could not be foreseen in the 1970s and that few borrowers thought, in those days, that they would face high interest rates so soon. Yet even though the specific turning point was certainly unforeseen, this does not imply that lending in the 1970s was made irrespective of *some* assumptions about a possible set of bad (perhaps, it was thought, idiosyncratic) circumstances that would switch the hierarchy between a nation's growth rate and world interest rates.

A simple way to represent (in retrospect) the shift from the 1970s to the 1980s is as follows. Assume that the world rate of interest is expected to oscillate between two values r_1 and r_2 along a given independently and identically distributed (i.i.d.) stochastic process. Call Z_1 the state of nature when the interest rate is r_1. Assume that $r_1 < n$. Call Z_2 the other state of nature and assume $r_2 > n$. Consider an economy inhabited by overlapping generations of the sort examined in section 2.1. Call $S(r)$ the savings of each member of the young generation. Assume $S(r_1) < 0$ and $S(r_2) > 0$.

As long as the economy stays in state 1, the trade balance becomes (in per capita of young generation terms)

$$TB_{11} = S(r_1) - \frac{1 + r_1}{1 + n} S(r_1) = \frac{n - r_1}{1 + n} S(r_1) < 0.$$

[This is exactly the case dealt with in equation (10) of section 2.2]. In contrast, when the economy shifts from state 1 into state 2, one has

$$TB_{12} = S(r_2) - \frac{1 + r_1}{1 + n} S(r_1) > 0.$$

The trade balance is the sum of the new savings $S(r_2)$ made by the young (they are positive by assumption) *plus* the repayment of their debt

$$\left(-\frac{1 + r_1}{1 + n} S(r_1) \right)$$

made by the old generations. It is necessarily positive.

If the economy then stays in state 2, one has

$$TB_{22} = S(r_2) - \frac{1 + r_2}{1 + n} S(r_2) = -\frac{r_2 - n}{1 + n} S(r_2) < 0.$$

Finally, if the economy moves back from state 2 to state 1, the trade balance becomes

$$TB_{21} = S(r_1) - \frac{1 + r_2}{1 + n} S(r_2),$$

which is, also, necessarily negative. As a result, in all instances but one the trade balance is negative. The country "almost" never repays its debt but for one circumstance: when the economy switches from low to high interest rates. In that case, all pressures add up to generate a trade balance surplus: the old generations repay their debt; the young generations want to save. With some optimism, this process may be viewed as one way to describe the shift from the 1970s to the 1980s, hence as a transitory phenomenon.

2.5 Conclusion

When lenders act rationally, borrowers should not (as a whole) have a free lunch, draining resources from the rest of the world without ever reversing the flow of payments. In a standard overlapping generations model, we have seen that it may take one generation before a borrowing nation starts reversing the flow of net transfers and gets locked, forever after, into a trade balance surplus.

In the case of the debt crisis of 1982, it was certainly less than a generation before the nations that borrowed in the mid-1970s were asked to service their debt. This may have come as a surprise to those (borrowers or private lenders) who predicted that the low interest rates of the 1970s would continue to prevail in the 1980s. Had such a prediction come true, debtors of the 1970s certainly would have kept draining resources from abroad. We have seen, however, that the switch to an equilibrium in which interest rates went above growth rates, while unquestionably a stochastic event, could not be ruled out with certainty. Rather than repeating the argument in this chapter, it is enough to emphasize that the *governments* of the debtor nations would have tried to borrow *more* if indeed they had expected to be able to drain net resources from abroad forever.

The switch of regime that occurred in the early 1980s was certainly unforeseen. Less than a decade after they started to borrow abroad, borrowers were suddenly asked to reverse their trade balances and repay their debts. But then, why should they? What would happen if the debtor nations simply refused to service their debt? The rest of this book explores the consequences of the answers to this question.

II THE RISK OF DEBT REPUDIATION

The temptation to repudiate one's debt is one that all borrowers in the world have experienced. Few actually do it, however. For an individual, refusing or being unable to pay his mortgage makes it likely that his house will be seized. For a firm, bankruptcy and the takeover of management by the lenders (bondholders or bankers) is the outcome of being unable to service its debt. In these two examples, the cost of defaulting on a debt is the loss of those properties that the lenders can take as collateral. How the lenders split this collateral among themselves is an important aspect (we shall see in chapter 4 that it plays an important role in assessing the efficiency of the loan market). It is, however, secondary to the crucial idea that lenders know that they can seize a tangible part of the borrower's wealth—indeed, in the case of a firm, all of the borrower's wealth—when the borrower defaults.

It is not *always* the case that debtors can use some or all of their properties as collateral for their debt. Certainly, students cannot use their human wealth as collateral for the loans they are granted, because the law against slavery forbids it. In those instances, the analysis would bear some analogy to the case of a sovereign debt that we now address.

Unlike a firm, a sovereign state cannot offer its lenders a credible collateral on its domestic capital. It may *pledge* to offer some piece of land in case of payment difficulties. To the extent that a sovereign state can change its domestic law as it likes, these pledges have no value (it can always, for example, impose a 100% property tax on the land it promised). In international affairs, the legal value of a contract does not carry the same weight as in domestic matters. When a firm cannot pay, banks or bondholders become—by law—the owners of the firm. When a country cannot pay, or simply refuses to, lenders have no (or few) supranational umpires to whom they can turn. This explains why most loans to a sovereign state cannot be collateralized. The only firm counterpart on which the lenders can rely is the threat of imposing sanctions on a defaulting country.

The following two chapters review many fundamental implications of this feature of international lending. The most crucial one is that the debt of a nation, even when it is contracted by private agents, is a public bad that the government wants to watch. Indeed, when the debt of the nation is large in the aggregate, the government can step in and increase the nation's welfare by allowing its private citizens to default on their external debt. In this absence of sanctions on the country as a whole, there are certainly instances in which private agents will be grateful to the government for keeping them from paying their foreign debt. This public-good nature of the debt of a nation explains why such a large part of the debt of LDCs is public or publicly guaranteed.

Another important feature of the debt to a nation is that both lenders and borrowers will have "ex-ante" incentives, which differ from the "ex-post" actions that they will want to take. Ex ante, the borrower will want the sanctions that the lender can impose in case of default to be large. Indeed, the larger the sanctions, the larger the loans. Ex post, obviously, it will want the sanctions to be mild.

Also ex ante, the lenders and the borrower may agree that they will not try to negotiate an agreement in case of debt difficulties. Ex post, however, it would be foolish to simply let the country default and trigger sanctions, which are a negative-sum game. These features and others offer a rich picture of loans to a sovereign state. Chapter 4 investigates the specific nature of the rescheduling of an LDC debt.

3 Capacity versus Willingness to Pay

In the previous part, I have shown that the trade balance of a nation should not be of specific concern to domestic policymakers or to foreign lenders. To the extent that world and domestic financial markets are functioning efficiently and are appropriately integrated, they impose upon *each* of a nation's members a budget constraint that yields (when aggregated) the nation's intertemporal trade balance equilibrium.

Now, any casual observation of the real world shows instead how important it is for Brazil or Mexico or any indebted *nation* to reach a trade balance target that fulfills financial market requirements. This is not meant to imply that domestic considerations are neglected, but that external considerations have a role of their own that cannot be subsumed by domestic factors. These "facts," if they are accepted, point to the inadequacy of the perfect capital market hypothesis. While there are a variety of ways to relax this hypothesis, I shall essentially focus, for the rest of this book, on only one of them: that which stems from the threat of external debt repudiation.

In this chapter and the one that follows, I want to model the implications (in the simple case when the economy is finitely lived) of this threat of debt repudiation on the functioning of credit markets. (The infinitely lived case will be examined in the following part.) I assume that repudiating its debt imposes a loss of efficiency on the defaulting country, and I examine the consequences of these threats for the lending and borrowing strategies available to the agents.

3.1 A Framework of Analysis

This chapter analyzes a two-period economy of the variety addressed in section 1.1. Here we shall simply assume that all agents (households, firms, and the government) live for two periods. Period 1 will be called the present, period 2, the future. As in the previous part, assume first that all firms and households have free access to the world financial markets. Call r the interest rate that prevails worldwide. Let us first briefly cast chapter 1's results in a two-period format.

3.1.1 Firms

Firm j decides in period 1 to make an investment I_{ij}. For the sake of simplicity we will disregard adjustment costs, capital depreciation, and labor so that in period 2 firm j may produce (f_j being the production function and K_{1j} the initial investment)

$$q_{2j} = f_j(K_{1j} + I_{1j}).$$

Each firm wants to pursue an investment program maximizing

$$W_j = \underset{I_{1j}}{\text{Max}} \ [f_j(K_{1j}) - I_{1j} + \frac{1}{1+r} f_j(K_{1j} + I_{1j})]. \tag{1}$$

The solution is given by the condition

$$f_j'[K_{1j} + I_{1j}] = 1 + r. \tag{2}$$

If the production functions f_j are identical across all firms, then all firms would have the same installed capital in period 2. If it is assumed that in period 1, the level of installed capital is already identical across firms (because in itself it resolves a prior optimization program), all firms may be aggregated into a one whose production technology is the sum of the individual technologies.

3.1.2 Households

Knowing the wealth accruing to him through ownership of firms, each consumer i can in turn come to the financial markets to invest his savings or borrow, in order to maximize

$$\text{Max } u(C_{1i}) + \beta u(C_{2i}), \tag{3}$$

under the constraint

$$C_{1i} + \frac{1}{1+r} C_{2i} \leqslant W_i, \tag{3'}$$

in which W_i is agent's i initial wealth.

The first-order condition may be written

$$u'(C_{1i}) = \beta(1 + r)u'(C_{2i}). \tag{4}$$

Call $C_1 = \sum C_{1i}$; $C_2 = \sum C_{2i}$; $W = \sum W_i$. In accordance with (3'), we may aggregate the budget constraints of the individual agents into

$$C_1 + \frac{1}{1+r} C_2 \leqslant W.$$

3.1.3   The Government as a Social Planner

Let us leave aside the issue of public good and assume that the government is a social planner that seeks to maximize:

$$U = \sum \theta_i u(C_{i1}, C_{i2}). \tag{5}$$

It is a standard exercise to show that there exists θ_i for which the planner's preferred outcome is the decentralized equilibrium.

In this chapter and the following one, we shall limit our view of the government to this behavior: that of a social planner, maximizing a social welfare function such as (5), that can costlessly impose whatever taxation or transfers it likes. At this stage, as long as credit markets work perfectly, nothing more needs to be done.

3.1.4   The Rest of the World

Let us now describe the country's overall balance of payments. In period 1, the trade balance is defined as

$$TB_1 = f(K_1) - I_1 - C_1. \tag{6}$$

It measures the difference between national output ($f(K_1)$) and national absorption ($C_1 + I_1$).

In period 2, the country's trade balance will likewise be written

$$TB_2 = f(K_1 + I_1) - C_2 \tag{7}$$

(there is no investment in period 2). From chapter 1, we know that

$$TB_1 + \frac{1}{1+r} TB_2 = 0.$$

3.2   The Possibility of Repudiating External Debt: Introduction

3.2.1   Benefits and Costs of Debt Repudiation

In period 2, households and firms have been repaid their claims or have repaid their debt. Let us assume that the country is a net borrower in period 1, so that, on aggregate, it must generate a trade surplus in period 2. What would happen if the government were to let its (*indebted*) citizens repudiate their debts? To the extent that international laws depend on their acceptance by sovereign states, foreign creditors need the government's assistance to recapture their claims. If the government is a social planner, acting on behalf of its constituency, it will have no reason to compel its citizens to repay their foreign debt if no retaliation from the creditors follows.

Even when the creditors can seize all assets belonging to residents of the country, repudiating its external debt will still be *collectively* preferable for the country if it is a *net* debtor. Only an additional *penalty* can deter the government from encouraging its citizens to repudiate their debt.

Throughout this chapter, I draw on the analysis of Eaton and Gersovitz (1981a and 1981b) and on my work with Jeffrey Sachs (Sachs and Cohen 1985, Cohen and Sachs 1986) in giving an operational content to this penalty. We will suppose that international lenders can inflict a loss upon any country that does not submit itself to international law, a loss that we shall assume to be proportionate to the country's income. This cost may be interpreted as the measure of the loss of productivity imposed on a country that flouts international law. For example, reprisal may take the form of limiting the supply of certain necessary raw materials—or any other form that would have the effect of reducing the country's income. In the model we have used, all of the country's income derives from firms' production. In analyzing the penalty, we shall simply assume that firms' production technology $f(\ )$ is reduced to

$$f_{ai}(K_i) = (1 - \lambda)f_i(K_i),$$

where f_{ai} is the output of firm i after the embargo by international creditors.

In the model we will study in the following chapter, the cost of defaulting will also include the indirect costs resulting from *financial* autarky. In the two-period model we consider here, only direct costs dictate the decision. Importantly, we shall assume that the cost $\lambda f = \lambda \sum_i f_i$ is *not* captured by the lenders. It is not a collateral; it is only a threat that lenders can impose on a country that fails to honor its international commitments.

3.2.2 Government Intervention

Based on this assumption, the external debt becomes a *public bad*. Any default on payment announced by a national borrower (protected by the national authorities) would result in a cost for all national producers.

Let D_i be the debt of each agent and R_i the repayment falling due in period 2. The national authorities will permit private agents to default on their payment if and only if

$$\sum R_i > \lambda \sum f_i(K_i). \tag{8}$$

The aggregate cost of repudiating the nation's overall debt must be smaller than the burden of honoring it. How will creditors deal with this externality? If the government does not centralize the debt, a simple way for lenders to avoid defaults is to insist that *each* firm's repayment satisfy

$$R_i \leqslant \lambda f_i(K_i). \tag{9}$$

If each lender is assured that each borrower is bound by a relationship such that (9), then the country will necessarily not default. However, a rule such as (9) may be very inefficient for the country. Some firms with very high productivity might wish to borrow beyond (9), while others would wish to borrow less, and yet the country could still satisfy (8). This inefficiency may be overcome by government intervention as is customary in an equilibrium with externality. For instance, the government may itself borrow on foreign markets and redistribute the product of its borrowing to national agents. How would this redistribution take place? One traditional way would be to impose an optimal tax on borrowing so as to spread the macroeconomic constraint (8) efficiently. Let us see how this taxation must be introduced.

Suppose that the authorities seek to maximize

$$\sum_i \theta_i [u(C_{1i}) + \beta u(C_{2i})], \tag{10}$$

under constraints

$$\sum_i C_{1i} + \frac{1}{1+r} \sum C_{2i} \leqslant \sum_j [f_j(K_j) - I_j] + \frac{1}{1+r} \sum_j f_j(K_j + I_j), \tag{11}$$

$$\sum_i C_i + \sum_j [I_j - f(K_j)] \leqslant \frac{\lambda}{1+r} \sum_j f_j(K_j + I_j). \tag{12}$$

The first inequality is the usual budget constraint. The second is the constraint that lenders will impose on the country to avoid repudiation on the country's solvency (in period 2, repayment $D(1 + r)$ must be smaller than the penalty for default). μ and γ are the Lagrange multipliers associated with these inequalities. The first-order conditions may be written

$$u'(C_{1i}) = \beta(1 + r)(1 + \tau)u'(C_{2i}); \qquad \tau = \frac{\gamma}{\mu},$$

$$f_j'(K_j + I_j) = \frac{1 + \tau}{1 + \tau\lambda}(1 + r).$$

(13)

The two conditions provide an immediate means of decentralizing the macroeconomic debt constraint. It suffices to impose an external consumer borrowing tax defined by the ratio of the two Lagrange multipliers associated respectively with the wealth constraint and the nonrepudiation constraint. Moreover, firms would have to be taxed on their external borrowing by a factor $[(1 + \tau/1 + \tau\lambda) - 1]$. With such taxation, the choice of consumption and investment by private agents can be optimally be decentralized, in accordance with the constraint that the debt will not be repudiated.

3.2.3 The Role of an Outside Agency in Coordinating External Debt between Borrower and Lender

The calculation of the optimal taxation scheme reveals a slight anomaly. The marginal cost of foreign borrowing is not the same for firms and consumers. Why is this so? A look at the nonrepudiation constraint provides the answer. The government wants to create a specific incentive for firms to invest in order to increase the volume of debt available to the country. Any additional investment increases the amount of lending available to the country by a factor $\lambda f'(K)/(1 + r)$ and loosens constraint (12). Hence it is not surprising that the marginal cost of loans contracted by firms is lower than that of households. However, this feature conceals a problem as to how the foreign loans are contracted. This problem is as follows.

In expressing the nonrepudiation constraint (12), we supposed that loan D was limited by the costs of repudiation, inclusive of those associated with the outcome of investment undertaken in period 1. For this to be so, bankers had to be certain that the investments would be made in line with equations (13). Let us assume that this is not the case and that bankers must *first* make loan D before the investment programs could be undertaken. How should loan D be calculated? The bankers will seek to determine the optimum use to which the borrower will put it. Let us assume that the government will try to maximize, as before, the following criterion:

$$\text{Maximize } \sum_i \theta_i [u(C_{1i}) + \beta u(C_{2i})], \tag{14}$$

under the constraints

$$\sum_i \left[C_{1i} + \frac{1}{1+r} C_{2i} \right] \leqslant \sum (f_j(K_j) - I_j) + \frac{1}{1+r} f_j(K_j + I_j)$$

and

$$\sum_i C_{1i} + \sum_j I_j - f(K_j) \leqslant D.$$

The second inequality tells us that the volume of lending in period 1 is limited by the amount D accorded by the banks.

If $\tau = \gamma/\mu$ is, as before, the ratio of the two Lagrange multipliers associated with debt and wealth, respectively, we now find that the following first-order conditions must hold to reach an efficient equilibrium:

$$u'(C_{1i}) = \beta(1+r)(1+\tau)u'(C_{2i}),$$
$$f_j'(K_j + I_j) = (1+r)(1+\tau). \tag{15}$$

We now see that foreign borrowing by households and firms entails the same marginal cost. The asymmetry between households and firms introduced above has been eliminated. The nature of the problem has changed. Under system (14) the country is subject to a rationing constraint, which is no longer contingent on its investment projects. Once the loans are granted, it is no longer optimal for the country to seek to invest so as to increase the amount of borrowing. If banks must make the first move, they will make due allowance for this in their calculations. Hence they will compute the amount of investment the country will make according to program (14) and extend loans that will satisfy

$$D \leqslant \frac{\lambda}{(1+r)} \sum_j f_j(K_j + I_j),$$

when I_j resolves problem (14) instead of problem (10).

This latter procedure is naturally inferior for the country to the first one we considered. But to attain the optimal program, the country must convince its bankers in advance that it will apply taxation program (13) and not program (14) (which would, however, be best once the loans had been granted). Here we can see the role that institutions such as the International Monetary Fund and the World Bank can play in such a situation. They can increase the supply of lending by explicitly linking the granting of new credits to the pursuit of the optimal program (13).

3.3 Strategic Relationships between Borrowers and Lenders

3.3.1 Bonds and Banks

As Sachs (1982) stressed in his historical study, one of the most important differences in international borrowing before and after World War II lies in the role played by the banks. Before World War II, the main international lending instrument was the bond market. Sachs argues that one of the prime characteristics of such a market is that it excludes negotiation between borrowers and lenders. This view is somewhat exaggerated, as pointed out by Eichengreen and Portes (1986), who show that bondholders did manage to act in a collectively efficient way. In this chapter, however, in order to contrast the two markets, we shall assume that lenders in a bond market are scattered and anonymous and that no agency can properly represent them. Thus a country that cannot honor its debt will have no option but to default. By contrast, we shall say that a credit market allows an insolvent debtor to negotiate with its creditors. A partial moratorium may be declared, enabling the country to honor only a part of its commitments without having to suffer the cost of repudiation. In the terms of our earlier model, the country will indeed always be willing to repay the cost λf that it would suffer were it to default.

This cooperative equilibrium is obviously "ex-post" Pareto-superior to unilateral debt repudiation. A net surplus (the cost λf imposed on a country declared to be in default) may be distributed among creditors and debtors. The way in which the split is decided depends on the outcome of the negotiatons between debtors and creditors. In any case, a Pareto-improvement can always be obtained by negotiation.

In the two-period model described in the previous section, the country's income in period 2 is known in advance in period 1. Creditors are thereby able to limit the amount of their lending to avoid default in period 2. Based on these assumptions, it is clear that a bond market and a credit market would yield the same outcome. In both cases, the same rationing constraint as in equation (8) would apply. The situation would be different if income in period 2 were unknown. In such a case, lenders would have to run the risk of nonrepayment in full of their claims in period 2. Let us now examine this case.

3.3.2 Introducing Uncertainty

Let us simplify the above framework by leaving aside all heterogeneity among consumers. With this hypothesis, the government (i.e., really, the social planner) wants to maximize the representative consumer's utility function:

$$U(C_1, C_2) = u(C_1) + \beta u(C_2).$$

We shall assume that u is homothetic, so that C_1 and C_2 can be taken to be aggregate rather than per capita consumption.

We will assume that the country's output is described by production Q_1 in period 1 and $\tilde{Q}_2$, a random variable, in period 2. The cumulative distribution of $\tilde{Q}_2$ is given by $F_2(Q_2)$, of which the support is $[0, \infty]$:

$$P[\tilde{Q}_2 \leqslant Q_2^*] = F_2(Q_2^*),$$

where the left-hand side measures the probability that output in period 2 will be below a threshold Q_2^*. We suppose that

$$F_2(Q_2) > 0, \qquad \forall Q_2 > 0.$$

In other words, we assume that any value Q_2 of output could be obtained in period 2. In the following sections we shall leave aside the question of investment.

3.3.3 The Risk of Debt Repudiation

Should the country *not* borrow, its expected utility level at the beginning of period 1 could be

$$U = u(Q_1) + \beta \int_0^\infty u(Q_2) dF_2(Q_2).$$

Let us now suppose that the country does borrow. Since we have supposed that the country's income may take any non-nil value (according to the distrbution F_2), we see the country will necessarily wish to default with a certain positive probability. Let D_1 be the initial debt contracted in period 1 and R_2 the repayments due in period 2.

When

$$\lambda Q_2 < R_2,$$

the country will prefer to repudiate its debt (and suffer cost λQ_2) rather than repay R_2. Call

$$Q_2^* = \frac{1}{\lambda} R_2.$$

The probability that the country will not repay in full the face value of its debt will be

$$\pi_2^* = F_2[Q_2^*].$$

3.3.4   Equilibrium on the Credit Market

To calculate the optimal amount of debt D^* that the country would wish to contract in period 1, we must first make an assumption as to how it will be repaid in period 2. In the case of a credit market, we suppose that the banks can ensure that the country will repay

$$R_2' = \lambda Q_2, \qquad \text{if } Q_2 < Q_2^*,$$

and

$$R_2' = R_2, \qquad \text{if } Q_2 \geqslant Q_2^*.$$

We thus assume that the banks can obtain the full repayment due to them if the country is solvent [in the sense of (8)] and, if not, obtain repayment of the full cost that the country would suffer were it to default.

Suppose that the banks are made up of lenders that are risk-neutral and that the credit market is a competitive one. If r is the opportunity cost of bank credit, these assumptions will imply that the supply of credit is determined solely by whether the expected value of bank profit is non-negative:

$$-D_1(1 + r) + \left\{ R_2(1 - \pi_2^*) + \int_0^{Q_2^*} \lambda Q_2 dF_2(Q_2) \right\} = 0. \tag{17}$$

This equation says that the opportunity cost of a bank credit $(-D_1(1 + r))$ must be offset on average by the repayments over period 2: R_2 with probability $(1 - \pi_2^*)$ and only λQ_2 for any value of Q_2 between 0 and $Q_2^* = (1/\lambda)R_2$.

Condition (17) may also be expressed as follows:

$$D_1 = \frac{1}{1+r} R_2 \left[1 - \pi_2 + \frac{1}{R_2} \int_0^{R_2/\lambda} \lambda Q_2 dF_2(Q_2) \right].$$ (18)

Call

$$\psi_2 \equiv \pi_2 - \frac{1}{R_2} \int_0^{R_2/\lambda} \lambda Q_2 dF_2(Q_2),$$ (19)

$$\psi_2(R_2) \equiv F_2 \left[\frac{R_2}{\lambda} \right] - \frac{1}{R_2} \int_0^{R_2/\lambda} \lambda Q_2 dF_2(Q_2),$$ (19′)

so that the supply of bank credit becomes

$$D_1 = \frac{1}{1+r} R_2 [1 - \psi_2(R_2)].$$ (20)

3.3.5 Credit and Bond Markets

Equation (20) relates credits supplied in period 1 to repayments due in period 2. Let us compare this equation with the one that would result were lending to be supplied via the bond market, on the same assumptions of lenders' risk-neutrality and competitive behavior:

$$-D_1(1 + r) + R_2(1 - \pi_2^*) = 0,$$ (21)

i.e.:

$$D_1 = \frac{1}{1+r} R_2 [1 - \pi_2(R_2)]; \qquad \pi_2(R_2) \equiv F_2 \left(\frac{R_2}{\lambda} \right).$$

In the case of bond lending, the probability of repayment is $1 - \pi_2^*$, and default would not give rise to any agreement between the borrower and his lenders.

Note that

(i) $\pi_2(R_2) \geqslant \psi_2(R_2)$

(ii) $\dfrac{d\psi_2(R_2)}{dR_2} = \dfrac{1}{R_2^2} \displaystyle\int_0^{R_2/\lambda} \lambda Q_2 dF_2(Q_2) \geqslant 0.$

From (i) we see that for the same repayment R_2 in period 2, bank credit supplies more funds in period 1. This argument shows the superiority of bank credit to the bond market. (Below we will discuss the changes in assumptions that could invalidate this finding.) From (ii) we see that ψ_2 and π_2 are positively correlated: both increase with R_2. We may hence interpret ψ_2 as an "adjusted" probability of default. The "adjustment" applies to the amount that would be repaid to the creditor should the borrower be unable to repay his debt in full.

3.3.6 Comparison of Credit and Bond Market Equilibria When the Country Has Some Power of Negotiation

It should be clear that the superiority of the credit market to the bond market outlined above is not a general result. Under certain circumstances, it may be the case that the borrower will wish to commit itself to *not* negotiating with its creditors: negotiations, indeed, may reduce—ex post— the repayment made by the borrower, but this would then reduce—ex ante—the amount of lending that the creditors are willing to offer. Let us examine in greater detail why such a scenario would occur if the country were given some bargaining power over its creditors.

In the equilibrium situation studied in the previous section, we assumed that creditors could force the country to repay the fraction λQ_2 of the amount owed. While this would improve the creditors' position, the debtors would be in precisely the same situation as if they had opted to default. Given this assumption, the debtor is devoid of any powers of negotiation. But if the indebted nation were to refuse the arrangements proposed, it would be neither better nor worse off, and the creditors would lose out. It thus seems reasonable to assume that the debtor will obtain a moratorium in period 2 that will be at least slightly superior to the one assumed earlier. I shall base my analysis on the position that would have pertained had the negotiation resulted in the equilibrium described by the Nash solution to the problem of bargaining. This concept was proposed by Nash in 1950 and yields an equilibrium outcome to bargaining between N agents. Each agent wields a threat, which is the autarkic utility available to him if negotiations founder. The negotiations concern which cooperative equilibrium will be selected. Take the example of negotiations between banks and the borrower. Should these break down, the noncooperative equilibrium would result in the country obtaining the autarkic equilibrium and the banks receiving nothing. Should the negotiations succeed, the banks would receive a fraction $\theta \lambda Q_2$ (θ being between zero and one) of the cost of default, and the country would consume $u[Q_2(1 - \lambda\theta)]$.

How should we select an equilibrium value of θ? Nash (1950) has proposed an equilibrium concept that is the solution to the following problem:

1) The cooperative equilibrium should not depend on the cardinal utility representation u_i of the agents. In other words, if the function u is transformed by a linear application, the solution to the problem must stay unchanged.

2) The equilibrium should depend "symmetrically" on each player in the following sense: if the players are identical in their utilities and their threats, the rule of negotiation should also yield a symmetric equilibrium.

3) There must be independence of the equilibrium vis-à-vis irrelevant alternatives. This axiom (which is the most debatable; see Roth 1979) states that the cooperative equilibrium would not be modified if players were offered the opportunity for further negotiations, which would not be taken up at equilibrium. In our example, the equilibrium should not be changed were one to add the possibility that banks could grant the country a unilateral transfer.

4) The cooperative equilibrium must be Pareto-optimal. This axiom is tantamount to assuming the players to be rational.

On these four assumptions on the nature of the equilibrium sought, Nash has shown that negotiation between N players was the solution to the following problem:

$$\text{Maximize } \prod_{i=1}^{N} [u_i(x_i) - u_i(d_i)],$$

where $C = \{x_i\}_{i=1\ldots N}$ is the point of agreement and $M = \{d_i\}_{i=1\ldots N}$ the autarkic point each player would obtain were agreement not reached. In a fundamental paper, Rubinstein (1982) has recently shown how a positive theory of sequential bargaining would reach the same conclusion as this axiomatic approach. Rubinstein's approach was taken to the LDC case by Bulow and Rogoff (1988).

In the case of a negotiation between a bank and a borrower, banks being risk-neutral, the Nash approach simply amounts to solving

$$\underset{\theta}{\text{Max}} \{u[(1 - \lambda\theta)Q_2] - u[(1 - \lambda)Q_2]\}\lambda\theta Q_2. \tag{22}$$

The first-order condition is then

$$-\lambda\theta Q_2 u'[(1 - \lambda\theta)Q_2] + u[(1 - \lambda\theta)Q_2] - u[(1 - \lambda)Q_2] = 0$$

or

$$u'[(1 - \lambda\theta)Q_2] = \frac{u[(1 - \lambda\theta)Q_2] - u[(1 - \lambda)Q_2]}{\lambda\theta Q_2}.$$

If the country is risk-neutral (just as its creditors), then

$$\theta = \frac{1}{2}.$$

In other words, the banker and the country share equitably the surplus λQ_2 accruing from the negotiation. Should the country, however, be risk-averse, then

$$\theta > \frac{1}{2}.$$

In this case, the country sets greater store by achieving an agreement than the bankers. The banker turns this to its advantage and obtains a better repayment by threatening not to agree to the arrangement.

Now let us look at the implications of negotiations along such lines between the country and its creditors. In period 2, the negotiations allow the country to obtain a fraction $(1 - \theta\lambda)Q_2$, $1/2 \leqslant \theta \leqslant 1$, of additional consumption. If the creditor has made an average nil profit, it will request in period 1 a rate of interest r_{12} such that

$$R_2 = (1 + r_{12})D_1 \tag{24}$$

and

$$-D_1 + \frac{1}{1 + r}(1 - \pi_2)R_2 + \frac{\theta}{1 + r}\int_0^{R_2/\lambda\theta} \lambda Q_2 dF_2(Q_2) = 0. \tag{25}$$

In the case in which $\theta = 1$, we find the equilibrium without negotiation reached in the previous section. Similarly, we may write, in the general case,

$$D_1 = \frac{1}{1 + r}R_2[1 - \psi_{2\theta}],$$

where

$$\psi_{2\theta} = \pi_2 - \frac{\lambda\theta}{R_2}\int_0^{R_2/\lambda\theta} Q_2 dF_2(Q_2).$$

The results of the previous section are thus entirely applicable providing that $\lambda\theta$ is replaced by θ. The lower θ is, the lesser the bankers' powers of negotiation. In the extreme case where $\theta = 0$, the bankers would enjoy no powers of negotiation in period 2. For this reason they would also lend nothing, since there would be no likelihood of any loan being repaid. By and large, the supply of bank credit is an incremental function of θ, banks' powers of negotiation. Hence, too, the country's utility function measured in period 1 becomes a *decreasing* function of the country's powers of negotiation in period 2. But this is obviously not the case in period 2. (In period 2, the greater the country's powers of negotiation, the better its position.) Thus in period 1 the country would clearly want to pledge not to use its possible negotiating powers in period 1, even though it would wish to use them later. Should creditors expect the country to act only in its own best interests when that time came, they would give no credence to the latter's assurances of good intentions. One way out of this dilemma would be to issue *bonds*. These are non-negotiable (assuming that the lenders are scattered and anonymous). In this case, if the value of θ expected by creditors is too low, the country could increase the supply of international loans by calling on the bond market. In this light, our earlier finding as to the superiority of the credit market may be questioned. Although the credit market derives an advantage from its superior negotiating capacities, it also suffers the drawbacks.

3.3.7 The Risk of Bank Panic

We will now show how the foregoing considerations shed fresh light on the problems of a bank panic. We have seen that the country's powers of negotiation are a major factor in determining the supply of lending. In our calculations we confined ourselves to the case of negotiations between a bank and a borrower. Let us now take the case in which several banks are involved in the negotiations. The Nash equilibrium continues to be written as the solution to problem (22). Let us suppose that all agents, including the borrower, are risk-neutral. In this case it may immediately be verified that the solution to the maximization problem (22) is

$$R_i = \frac{1}{N}\lambda Q_2; \qquad C_2 = \left[1 - \lambda\frac{N-1}{N}\right]Q_2.$$

Each creditor receives a share $1/N$ of λQ_2, which is under negotiation. The debtor country may itself increase its consumption of $1/N\ \lambda Q_2$ relative to autarky. Here each player is perfectly symmetrical and receives the same fraction of the return yielded by a cooperative agreement. This solution to the Nash problem given in (22) nonetheless does not entirely address our dilemma. The repayment to each creditor is indeed unrelated to the face value of the claims held, due to creditors' risk-neutrality. But (legally) they cannot receive more than the nominal amount to which they are entitled. Thus creditor i would get

$$R'_i = \text{Max}[R_i, R_{0i}],$$

where R_i is the outcome of the negotiations as formally calculated above, and R_{0i} is the face value of its claims. When $R_{0i} > R_i$, creditor i will be repaid in full, with the other creditors redistributing the remainder in the same way. Thus a marginal lender (relative to all other lenders) may obtain full repayment of the claim he holds, even when all others obtain only partial repayment. The intuition underlying this somewhat paradoxical outcome (which is consistent, however, with the course of interbank negotiations) is the following: The Nash equilibrium measures the power of each participant in terms of the difference between the outcome of the negotiations and the threat (the autarkic equilibrium) exerted by those who contest the outcome. In this instance the hand of small lenders is strengthened by the fact that breaking off negotiations would cost them less than it would the larger creditors.

The negotiating rules I have described work in favor of small lenders and encourage each creditor to hold only a small fraction of the total loan. But this raises the specter of a bank panic: if no one wishes to hold more than a small fraction of the total, the total could be nil. If I am expecting no other creditor, I lend nothing, and if we all take the same line of reasoning, the supply of credit could dwindle to zero. Let us take as an example a country with a two-period lifespan, which has already inherited at the start of period 1 a debt contracted in earlier periods. Suppose the country is risk-neutral: its utility function is worth

$$U(C_1, C_2) = C_1 + \frac{1}{1 + \delta} C_2.$$

The constraint regarding further lending is

$$D_1(1 + r) \leqslant \lambda \theta_N Q_2, \tag{26}$$

where $\theta_N = N/(N + 1)$ and depends on the number N of lenders in period 1. (When the number of lenders tends to infinity, the country's powers of negotiation are fully diluted, and we find the rationing constraint encountered earlier.) The country's utility becomes

$$U(D_0) = \text{Max } U(C_1, C_2),$$

subject to

$$C_1 + \frac{1}{1 + r} C_2 = Q_1 + \frac{1}{1 + r} Q_2 - D_0,$$

$$D_1 = -[Q_1 - D_0(1 + r) - C_1] \leqslant \frac{\lambda \theta_N}{1 + r} Q_2.$$

If the rate of time perference δ is greater than the international interest rate r, the country will seek to borrow to the hilt in period 1. Constraint (26) would apply, giving the following utility function level:

$$U(D_0) = \left[Q_1 - D_0(1 + r) + \frac{\lambda}{1 + r} \theta_N Q_2 \right] + \frac{1}{1 + \delta} [Q_2(1 - \theta_N)],$$

that is,

$$U(D_0) = Q_1 + \frac{1}{1 + \delta} Q_2 - D_0(1 + r) + \lambda \theta_N Q_2 \frac{\delta - r}{(1 + r)(1 + \delta)}.$$

When $\delta < r$ (the country being a borrower), it may be checked that the country's utility increases with θ_N, that is, commensurately with the banks' powers of negotiation.

Function $U(D_0)$ calculated above assumes that that the country is willing to repay its initial debt D_0. This would be the case were it assumed that

$$U(D_0) \geqslant U_a = (1 - \lambda) \left[Q_1 + \frac{1}{1 + \delta} Q_2 \right].$$

The right-hand side measures the utility obatined when the country has repudiated its debt and is bound by the autarkic consumption program $(C_1, C_2) = (1 - \lambda)(Q_1, Q_2)$. This condition may hence be expressed as

$$D_0 \leqslant \frac{\lambda}{1 + r} \left\{ Q_1 + \frac{1}{1 + \delta} Q_2 + \theta_N Q_2 \frac{\delta - r}{(1 + \delta)(1 + r)} \right\}.$$

The higher the values of λ and θ, the more unlikely debt repudiation will be. Let $h(\theta)$ be the right-hand side of this inequality. To express the possibility of a bank panic, we shall take the following case:

$$h(\theta_1) < D_0 \leqslant h(\theta_{N_0}),$$

for a value $N_0 \geqslant 2$. In this case the country would prefer to default if only one banker were willing to grant it further credit, but it would opt to honor its debt were a sufficient number N_0 of bankers ready to extend additional funds. Such a situation can lead to a bank panic. Should the new lenders fear that the quorum N_0 will not be achieved, nobody would wish to lend anything more to the country, which would then be impelled to repudiate its debt.

3.4 Conclusion

Allowing for the possibility of repudiation of external debt considerably alters our analysis of a nation's balance of payments. The strategic relationships between debtor and creditor can no longer be analyzed in the way suggested by financial theory in the previous chapters. Lenders must now explicitly appraise the *nation's* options and not only each of its member's budget constraints. We have shown how an outside agency such as the IMF may improve this relationship between lenders and borrower when the latter wishes to precommit itself to an investment program.

Our analysis in this chapter has shown that a nation's external debt is a public bad, justifying the government's involvement in any negotiations or refinancing arrangements. These powers of negotiation can, however, cause serious difficulties. It can sometimes reduce the amount the banks are prepared to lend. It may even create the conditions for a bank panic when the value of any single banker's claim depends on the participation of a sufficient number of other lenders. We now turn more specifically to the economic consequences of this public bad dimension of the threat of debt repudiation.

4 Voluntary and Involuntary Lending

In the previous chapter, the issue of debt repudiation was narrowed down to a simple question: should a debtor default rather than transferring to its lenders what they ask for? For the borrower (and for the lenders trying to guess its reaction), this is a one-shot decision that simply involves the borrower comparing the direct cost of debt repudiation to the service of the debt. In practice, however, the problem at hand is never so simple: the borrower can ask for new loans on the financial markets and—if it cannot get any—it can ask its previous lenders to reschedule the debt falling due, postponing to a later time the key question: pay or default?

Is it a good thing for banks to reschedule the debt (i.e., to postpone the repayment falling due) of a country that *cannot* generate the cash that is required, whether through a trade balance surplus or through access to the world financial markets?

The basic answer I offer is as follows. *Ex post*, at the time of the rescheduling, it may not make any difference whether lenders reschedule the debt that cannot be paid or simply write off enough of the debt to allow the country to tap the financial markets again. (See chapter 9 for a more specific answer in the context of an infinitely lived economy.)

Ex ante, however, we shall see that a basic inefficiency may arise when lenders and borrower cannot agree on how much new money the borrower will be entitled to raise on the financial markets. The origin of this inefficiency will appear to be directly related to the public bad dimension of the external debt. Unlike a firm, a nation cannot promise to pay some lenders and default on others. Default is a decision that triggers legal sanctions irrespective of the amount due. (Or more to the point: a whole set of legal sanctions can be triggered irrespective of the amount due. See, for example, the sanctions on Iran that U.S. banks were able to impose in 1979 due to a few million dollars in late payments.) Because of this, any new debt raised by the debtor increases the probability of default and dilutes the value of all senior debts. In reponse, senior lenders will lend too little, on a too short-term basis.

Firms can avoid this inefficiency because they can grant seniority privileges to senior lenders. Indeed, when a firm goes bankrupt, lenders line up to grasp whatever value of the firm they can get, a practice they cannot employ for a defaulting nation. New lenders to a firm are therefore offered (if the senior lenders are cautious enough to protect themselves) a contract that stipulates that in the case of bankruptcy they will be paid *after* the senior lenders. Those covenants create a specific market for marginal loans. Such a market cannot exist for a nation's debt. The difference between the average and the marginal value of a nation's debt will therefore appear to be a critical element of the analysis. It is given an empirical content in section 4.5. The implications of this analysis for a donor that wants to help an indebted nation are examined in the last part of this chapter.

4.1 A Framework of Analysis

4.1.1 A Three-Period Model

Let us assume that the nation lives for three periods. Period 1 is the present, period 2 is the short run, and period 3 is the long run. The country borrows D_1 in period 1; the service of D_1 over period 2 and 3 is named R_{12} and R_{13}. When $R_{12} = 0$, we shall call the debt long term. When $R_{13} = 0$, we shall call it short term. At time 2, the country may decide to go to the financial markets again and borrow D_2, which is associated with repayment R_{23} at time 3. Let us call (Q_1, Q_2, Q_3) the resources the country is endowed with in the three periods. If payment and endowment were deterministic, then the country would consume

$$\begin{cases} C_1 = Q_1 + D_1 \\ C_2 = Q_2 - R_{12} + D_{23} \\ C_3 = Q_3 - R_{13} - R_{23}. \end{cases}$$

Following the two-period model spelled out in the previous section, I now make the following assumptions:

1. At time 1, when the borrowing decision is made, Q_1 is known (to the country and to the lenders), but Q_2 and Q_3 are two independent random variables drawn from a probability distribution whose laws of repartition are $F_2(Q_2)$ and $F_3(Q_3)$, respectively.

2. If the country defaults at time 2, its endowment at times 2 and 3 is scaled down to $(1 - \lambda)Q_2$ and $(1 - \lambda)Q_3$, respectively. In addition, the country is barred from the financial markets. If the country defaults at time 3, its output is scaled down to $(1 - \lambda)Q_3$.

3. The country has no bargaining power, so that, at each point in time, the lenders can make credible take-it-or-leave-it offers.

4. The country is managed by a social planner who maximizes $E_0[u(C_1) + \beta u(C_2) + \beta^2 u(C_3)]$.

5. The world interest rate is constant, r; lenders are risk-neutral and act competitively.

Accepting these hypotheses, let us examine the equilibrium that is attained by the country. To arrive at the best strategy open to the country, we solve the model by backward induction. Taking as given the financial commitment made by the country during the previous periods, we must uncover the best available strategy from any time on.

4.1.2 Equilibrium in Period 3

When the country reaches period 3, if it has not yet defaulted in period 2, it owes R_{13} to its senior lenders and R_{23} to its junior lenders. If $\lambda Q_3 > R_{13} + R_{23}$, the country will not choose to repudiate its debt (for this is too costly, and the country has no bargaining power), so its consumption is

$$C_3 = Q_3 - (R_{13} + R_{23}).$$

If $\lambda Q_3 < R_{13} + R_{23}$, then the country would rather default than pay its debts. I assume, in this case, that junior and senior lenders can collude and suggest that the country repay only λQ_3. I further assume that they share among themselves those proceeds according to the face value of the claims. Senior lenders receive

$$R'_{13} = \frac{R_{13}}{R_{13} + R_{23}} \lambda Q_3,$$

while junior lenders receive

$$R'_{23} = \frac{R_{23}}{R_{13} + R_{23}} \lambda Q_3.$$

We let $\pi_3 = F_3[(R_{13} + R_{23})/\lambda]$ be the probability that the lenders are not repaid in full in period 3.

Period 3 is therefore very similar to the second period of the model examined in the previous chapter. The country must choose to default or pay, and the lenders gauge how much the country should pay given the threat of debt repudiation. We now analyze what happens in period 2, when the country has other options available.

4.2 Lending and Rescheduling

During period 2, the country finds out the value Q_2 of its resources and must decide whether to repay or not repay R_{12} to its period-1 creditors. Several options are available: 1. it can borrow D_{23} on the international markets and consume $C_2 = Q_2 - R_{12} + D_{23}$; 2. it can repudiate its debt and consume $C_2 = (1 - \lambda)Q_2$; or 3. it can turn to its period-1 creditors and demand a rescheduling of payment R_{12}.

4.2.1 New Lending

If the country chooses to pay R_{12} and borrow again on the international markets, it will have to solve the following problem:

$$\underset{D_{23}}{\text{Maximize}} \left\{ u(Q_2 - R_{12} + D_{23}) + \beta \int_{Q_3^*}^{\infty} u(Q_3 - \lambda Q_3^*)dF_3(Q_3) \right.$$

$$\left. + \beta \int_0^{Q_3^*} u[Q_3(1 - \lambda)]dF_3(Q_3) \right\},$$

where $Q_3^* \equiv 1/\lambda(R_{13} + R_{23})$ is the threshold defined in the preceding section. R_{23} is determined in such a manner that

$$-D_{23} + \frac{1}{1 + r} E_2 P_{23} = 0, \tag{5}$$

where

$$\begin{cases} P_{23} = R_{23} \text{ if } \lambda Q_3 \geqslant (R_{13} + R_{23}) \equiv \lambda Q_3^* \\[2mm] P_{23} = \dfrac{R_{23}}{R_{13} + R_{23}} \lambda Q_3, \quad \text{if } Q_3 < Q_3^*. \end{cases} \tag{6}$$

Equations (5) and (6) can also be written

$$(1 + r)D_{23} = [1 - F_3(Q_3^*)]R_{23} + \frac{R_{23}}{R_{13} + R_{23}} \int_0^{Q_3^*} \lambda Q_3 dF_3(Q_3),$$

or

$$\begin{cases} D_{23}(1 + r) = (1 - \psi_3^*)R_{23}, \\[2mm] \text{where} \\[2mm] \psi_3 = F_3(Q_3^*) - \dfrac{1}{Q_3^*} \int_0^{Q_3^*} Q_3 dF_3(Q_3). \end{cases} \tag{7}$$

ψ_3 is the analog to ψ_2 defined in equation (19) of the two-period model in the previous chapter.

The first-order condition of problem (4) then becomes

$$u'(C_2)\left(1 - \pi_2 - R_{13}\frac{d\psi_3}{dQ_3}\right) = \beta(1 + r)\int_{Q_3^*}^{\infty} u'(Q_3 - \lambda Q_3^*)dF_3(Q_3). \tag{8}$$

Let $U_2(Q_2, R_{12}, R_{13})$ be the utility value reached by the country in period 2 if it chooses the program (which I assume to be unique) that solves this equation (which I assume to be sufficient). U_2 is therefore defined by

$$U_2(Q_2, R_{12}, R_{13}) = \underset{D_{23}}{\text{Max}} \left\{ u(Q_2 - R_{12} + D_{23}) + \beta \int_{Q_3^*}^{\infty} u(Q_3 - \lambda Q_3^*)dF_3 \right.$$

$$\left. + \beta \int_0^{Q_3^*} u[(1 - \lambda)Q_3]dF_3(Q_3) \right\}. \tag{9}$$

The country will prefer default to choosing the market solution described by equation (9) if

$$U_{2,a}(Q_2) \equiv u[(1 - \lambda)Q_2] + \beta \int_0^{\infty} u[(1 - \lambda)Q_3]dF_3(Q_3)$$

$$\geqslant U_2(Q_2, R_{12}, R_{13}) \tag{10}$$

For bankers, unilateral default is a net loss, and they will invariably prefer rescheduling debt R_{12} to allowing the country to default.

4.2.2 Rescheduling

The rescheduling of debt R_{12} can in turn take three different forms:

1. The banks cancel the debt R_{13} and request immediate payment of R_{12}'. Once the moratorium is granted, the country is free to borrow on the international financial markets and to raise a loan D_{23} that will be a solution to (9) when R_{12} is substituted for R_{12}', and $R_{13} = 0$.

2. The banks reschedule the debt by requesting repayments R_{12}' today and R_{13}' tomorrow. Once the rescheduling is agreed to, the country is allowed to borrow on the international markets.

3. As in 2, bankers reschedule the debt, but the country is *not* free to borrow on the international markets after the agreement has been reached.

In appendix A, I demonstrate the following proposition:

PROPOSITION 1: The three rescheduling options are equivalent for the bankers. In 2, the bankers will necessarily choose $R_{13}' = 0$.

In other words, the bankers will all receive the same average repayment under each of the three agreements. However, Proposition 1 also indicates that the optimal rescheduling of 2 is the moratorium of 1. *It is therefore suboptimal for a banker to attempt to collect a debt R_{13} in period 3 if the country is free to turn to the international financial markets after the agreement has been reached.* The reasoning behind this statement is extremely simple. Once the agreement has been reached, the country will seek to increase the risk of defaulting in period 3 with respect to the optimal risk that would be calculated by the banker under the terms of a type-3. agreement. This is because, by increasing the risk, the country indirectly transfers a share of the value of the R'_{13} debt to its new bankers in exchange for higher credit today. To avoid this risk, the banks will want to deny the country access to the international financial markets. However, Proposition 1 demonstrates that this degree of freedom is illusory. Rescheduling is in fact tantamount to a partial moratorium, followed by the country's free access to international markets.

Let $J_2(Q_2, R_{12}, R_{13})$ be the utility resulting for the country in period 2 after rescheduling (if required), that is

$$J_2(Q_2, R_{12}, R_{13}) = \text{Sup}\left\{U_2(Q_2, R_{12}, R_{13}), U_{2,a}(Q_2)\right\}. \tag{11}$$

U_2 and $U_{2,a}$ are defined in (9) and (10).

For simplicity's sake, we shall assume that there always exists a threshold $Q_2^*(R_{12}, R_{13})$ such that

$$U_2(Q_2, R_{12}, R_{13}) \geqslant U_{2,a}(Q_2) \Leftrightarrow Q_2 \geqslant Q_2^*(R_{12}, R_{13}).$$

4.3 The Inefficiency of Private Lending to Sovereign States

Let us now show that the outcome generated in period 1—when all subsequent developments explained above are perfectly expected—is socially inefficient. The decision to borrow a certain amount D_1 in period 1 can itself be subdivided into two phases. The first phase consists of seeking the optimal repayment maturity for any amount D_1 borrowed. The second phase is to choose the optimal level D_1 itself. The first phase can be described as the solution of the program

$$J_1(D_1) = \max_{R_{12}, R_{13}} \int_0^\infty J_2(Q_2, R_{12}, R_{13}) dF_2(Q_2), \tag{12}$$

subject to the constraint

$$D_1 = E_1 \left\{ \frac{P_{12}}{1+r} + \frac{P_{13}}{(1+r)^2} \right\},$$

where P_{12} and P_{13} are the actual repayments corresponding to commitments R_{12} and R_{13}, calculated in the manner set out in section 4.2; $J_2(Q_2, R_{12}, R_{13})$ is the utility function, defined in equation (1), available to the country when the level of its endowments during the period is Q_2.

The second phase of the country's decision making in period 1 is quite simply

$$\underset{D_1}{\text{Maximize}}\; u(Q_1 + D_1) + \beta J_1(D_1).$$

We assume that there exists a unique solution $D_1^* > 0$ that is the solution to

$$u'(Q_1 + D_1^*) = -\beta J_1'(D_1^*). \tag{13}$$

We propose to demonstrate that the equilibrium thus obtained, which we define as the "market equilibrium," is inefficient.

PROPOSITION 2:   The market equilibrium defined above is inefficient.

The market equilibrium is defined by backward induction. In each period, the country's decision is always the best possible one, given the constraints imposed by the credit supply. Appendix B demonstrates that the equilibrium thus obtained could be improved with respect to period 1 if the country could commit itself to a borrowing strategy $D_{23}^*(Q_2)$ in period 2 that did not correspond to the market strategy defined in section 4.2. This strategy $D_{23}^*(Q_2)$ will nevertheless leave the country free to choose default. It is therefore not a strategy that restrains the country from defaulting when it wishes to do so. On the contrary, it is a strategy that commits the country to *reducing* its desired borrowing in period 2. By shrinking that amount, the optimal strategy will allow a reduction in debt D_1 risk, and this tradeoff will prove to be optimal with respect to period 1.

Proposition 2 illustrates the "time inconsistency" of economic policy choices: the optimal ex-ante policy is not optimal ex post. The potential existence of this property has been brought to light by Kydland and Prescott (1977) and Calvo (1978). For an application of this issue to public debt management, see also Persson and Svensson 1984, and Persson, Persson, and Svensson 1987.

4.4 The Market for Marginal Loans

4.4.1 Average and Marginal Prices of the Debt

The inefficiency of the credit market is intrinsically a by-product of the public bad dimension of the debt. To see this, let us first consider the market value of the debt when the country has reached period 2 and owes R_{13} to the senior lenders and R_{23} to the junior lenders.

Call $R = R_{13} + R_{23}$ the overall face value of the country's outstanding commitment. At the end of time 2, the market value of R can be aggregated into

$$V = \frac{1}{1+r} \int_0^{Q^*} \lambda Q_3 dF_3(Q_3) + \frac{1}{1+r} \int_{Q^*}^{\infty} R dF(Q_3), \tag{14}$$

in which

$$Q^* = \frac{1}{\lambda} R.$$

If all lenders were merging into a single one, the value—to this aggregate lender—of one more dollar due in period 3 would simply be measured as

$$q_m = \frac{\partial V}{\partial R} = \frac{1}{1+r} \int_{Q^*}^{\infty} dF_3(Q_3) = \frac{1}{1+r} [1 - F_3(R/\lambda)]. \tag{15}$$

This marginal price, however, is not the value of one more dollar accruing to an *individual* lender. It is therefore not the price observed on a secondary market on which the debt may be traded. This observed price is the average price, to the extent indeed that all lenders are treated symmetrically when the debt falls due.

This average price is simply

$$q = \frac{V}{R} = \frac{1}{1+r} \left[\int_0^{Q^*} \lambda \frac{Q_3}{R} dF_3(Q_3) + \int_{Q^*}^{\infty} dF_3(Q_3) \right]. \tag{16}$$

Taking the value of the marginal price q_m as it is defined in equation (15), one finds

$$q = q_m + \frac{1}{1+r} \int_0^{Q^*} \frac{\lambda Q_3}{R} dF_3(Q_3).$$ (17)

The average price is systematically above the marginal price of the debt. Why is this discrepancy a source of market inefficiency? To answer this question, let us see how this discrepancy would be dealt with in the case of corporate debt.

4.4.2 Average and Marginal Corporate Debt

Let us assume that the nation is a firm that is expected to generate profits $\pi \equiv \lambda Q_3$. If the firm owes R, then the market value of this debt is identical to the one obtained in equation (14). As long as profits are above R, lenders are paid in full (and the shareholders get whatever remains). When profits go below R, bondholders take over the company and distribute among themselves whatever profit π is generated. The basic difference between the debt of a company and that of a nation, however, is that bondholders may negotiate ex-ante property rights to a firm's collateralized capital in the event that it goes bankrupt.

It is therefore possible for the senior lenders to design a contract that grants them priority rights to the firm's profits should it become insolvent. However much money the firm borrows later, the new lenders know that they will be paid second. Contrary to what happens with sovereign debt, junior lenders are willing to pay only the marginal price, q_m, for one dollar that the firm may want to promise to pay in the future. Because the market for a marginal dollar correctly prices its value, it is easy to see why lending is efficient in the case of a corporate debt.

4.4.3 The Debt of a Nation

In the case of sovereign debt, in contrast, junior lenders are willing to pay the average value—not the marginal value—for an additional dollar owed by the country. This is a good deal for the country, and it explains why the country "overborrowed" in the second period.

One way for the senior lenders to avoid this inefficiency is to find ways to keep the country from tapping new lenders. How can that be done? Assume for instance that the country pledges not to tap new lenders in the future and to rely on its senior lenders for new funds (henceforth correctly priced at this marginal value). How can this pledge be made credible? The only means the lenders can come up with is to write the debt contract in such a way as to deter the borrower from reneging on its promise. Assume for the sake of argument that the repayment R_{12} is made contingent upon the new loans that the country may raise, and say that $R_{12} = +\infty$ if new lenders step in. With such a contract, the country is certainly kept from borrowing fresh loans on the financial markets and—in principle—the borrower can be forced to abide by its pledge.

In the real world, no such contracts are ever written, but banks have managed to maintain relatively collusive behavior, which has kept *some* (but certainly not all) bankers from free-riding on the others.

4.5 Average and Marginal Price of the Debt: An Empirical Estimate

4.5.1 The Elasticity of Secondary Market Prices

In this section I want to characterize empirically the difference between the marginal and the average price of the debt, such as it could be estimated from the behavior of the secondary market in 1987.

Let q be the average price of the debt and V its market value. One can write

$$V = qD. \tag{18}$$

The marginal value of the debt can therefore be written

$$q_m = \frac{\partial V}{\partial D} = q + D\frac{\partial q}{\partial D}. \tag{19}$$

Call ε the absolute value of the elasticity of the average price with respect to the face value of the debt. One can write

$$q_m = q[1 - \varepsilon]. \tag{20}$$

Characterizing the marginal price therefore amounts to calculating the (absolute value of the) elasticity of the average price with respect to the face value of the debt. It is this elasticity that we now want to calculate. In particular, we shall be interested in finding those countries for which the marginal value of the debt is zero and possibly negative (this oddity corresponds to the case in which there is a "debt Laffer curve" problem: this notion, proposed by Krugman, is discussed in chapter 9).

4.5.2 Empirical Estimate of Elasticity

Previous attempts to measure the elasticity of the price of the debt with respect to its nominal value systematically rendered a low estimate. A study by Purcell and Orlanski (1988), following a previous estimate by Sachs and Huizinga (1987), reported an elasticity of 0.34. I have estimated an equation representative of these earlier studies as follows:

$$\text{Log } q = 5.06 - 0.653 \text{ Log } D/X - 2.231 \, A/D - 1.016 \, R/D$$
$$\phantom{\text{Log } q = 5.06 - } (0.152) \qquad\qquad (0.603) \qquad\quad (0.373)$$

$$- 0.274 \text{ Dummy } 1987.12$$
$$ (0.132) \tag{21}$$

$R = 0.560$ Pooled equations for 1986.12 and 1987.12 data. 60 degrees of freedom. (Standard errors in parentheses.)

q = average price of the debt (cents on the dollar)

D = debt; X = exports; A = arrears;

R = amount of rescheduling performed since 1982.

From this equation, one would tend to accept at the 95% degree of confidence level that the elasticity of the debt was smaller than one, that is, that the marginal price of the debt is positive. Before commenting on the insufficiency of such an equation, it is interesting to report that the price of the debt seems to be very poorly correlated to macroeconomic data related to the country. For instance, the most important of these macroeconomic data, the noninterest current account—or the domestic rate of inflation, as another example—never appeared to be significantly correlated to the price. On the other hand, arrears or rescheduling [as we can see from equation (21)] always perform very well.

These results tend to indicate that the market is extremely sensitive to the punctuality of payments and pays little attention to overall macroeconomic performances. Finally, one also sees from equation (21) that a dummy separating the 1986 and 1987 data appears to be significant. This may be a reflection of Citibank's decision to build up $3 billion in reserves, a move that significantly influenced the market.

Despite its appeal and its simplicity, an equation such as (21) is extremely misleading. First, it leads to a rejection of the hypothesis that the elasticity of the price with respect to debt is larger than one for the entire sample. But it may very well be the case that only a subgroup of countries was hit by the debt overhang problem. Running the same regression for the subsample of 16 countries for which the debt-to-export ratio is larger than 3 yields a larger elasticity, which I estimated to be 1.183 (with a standard error of 0.339). Second, and perhaps more important, an equation such as (21) takes the arrears and the rescheduling variables as exogenous, although these variables obviously depend debt and perhaps on the price itself. To overcome these two difficulties (to which one should also add a more technical one, which is that of the price being smaller than 100, so that $\log q$ cannot be normally distributed), I have estimated a reduced-form equation in which the dependent variable has the logistic form $\log (q/100 - q)$, so as to let the elasticity depend on the price level. The result is as follows:

$$\text{Log} \frac{q}{100 - q} = \underset{(0.378)}{2.152} - \underset{(0.305)}{1.509} \text{Log } D/X - \underset{(0.024)}{0.048} X \text{ growth}$$

$$- \underset{(0.288)}{0.583} \text{Dummy 87.12} \tag{22}$$

$R = 0.389$. Pooled equation for 1986.12 and 1987.12 data.

60 degrees of freedom. X growth = rate of growth of exports.

4.5.3 Implications

According to this equation, price elasticity with respect to debt is 1.509 $(1 - q/100)$ with a standard error of 0.305. Table 4.1 indicates the countries for which the marginal price could *not* be accepted to be positive at various degrees of confidence. At the 90% degree of confidence level, only four countries pass the test.

For these countries, more nominal debt reduces the market value of the debt. For these "debt overhang" countries, it is counterproductive to have more claims than fewer (see chapter 9).

Let us now consider, along equation (22), those countries for which the marginal price is not significantly different from zero. $q_m = \varepsilon(1 - q)$ so that, at the $x\%$ degree of confidence, q_m cannot be significantly accepted as strictly positive as long as $\varepsilon = 1.509(1 - q) \geqslant 1 - t_x\sigma$ in which t_x is the t-statistic corresponding to the $x\%$ degree of confidence and $\sigma = 0.305$ is the standard error of the elasticity in equation (22).

Table 4.1
Debt overhang countries (the prices in parentheses are cents per dollar)

At the 50% level of	Argentina	(34)
confidence: $q \leqslant 34$	Jamaica	(33)
	Nigeria	(29)
At the 75% level of	Dominican Republic	(23)
confidence: $q \leqslant 23$	Congo	(23)
	Zaire	(19)
	Zambia	(17)
	Costa Rica	(15)
At the 90% level of	Bolivia	(11)
confidence: $q \leqslant 11$	Peru	(7)
	Nicaragua	(4)
At the 95% level of	Sudan	(2)
confidence: $q = 0$		

At the 95% degree of confidence level, only those countries for which the price of the debt is above 68 cents on the dollar exhibit a positive marginal price. At this level of confidence, from the group of HICs, only Colombia and Turkey are candidates. For all of the others, one cannot deny that the face value of the debt would not change the amount that the lenders expect the country to pay. *In the case of Brazil, for instance, even a 30% write-off would not significantly change the market value of the debt.* These results may be interpreted as a confirmation of the idea that lenders should not be expected to change the service of the debt, even (in Brazil's case) after the debt has been written down by a third of its value.

In this section, I simply want to discuss some of the policy debates that have been generated by these large discounts.

4.6   Implications for a Donor that Wants to Help an Indebted Nation

The market value of the debt of many LDCs decreased dramatically in the late 1980s. For some countries, such as Sudan and Bolivia, the market value of one dollar owed by the countries fell to almost zero. The previous econometric estimate of the determinants of the secondary market suggests that the marginal price of many LDC debts are not statistically different from zero. This is certainly a case in which no new loans should be offered to the country, whatever the risk premia might be.

The existence of such large discounts has many implications, in particular when lenders wish to take care of the counterincentive effect they may have on growth. Some of those problems are reviewed in chapters 8 and 9. Here I simply review how these discounts should be acknowledged by those who want to help LDCs reduce their debt.

4.6.1 Intervening on the Secondary Markets

Many proposals to help the indebted LDCs have suggested that the industrialized countries intervene on the secondary markets. The ICs would repurchase LDC debts at a low market price to relieve the indebted countries from having to pay the difference between the face and the market value of their debt. (Such a proposal has been fully articulated by James Robinson, chairman of American Express, among others.) The vehicle for such interventions would be an international agency that would be appropriately endowed by the industrialized countries for intervention on the secondary markets.

However generous it may be, such a proposal is bound to be counterproductive for at least two reasons. One has been emphasized by Bulow and Rogoff (1988) and hinges on the distinction between average and marginal pricing spelled out above. When intervening on the secondary markets, the international agency would have to pay the average price for a dollar whose value to the lenders, the marginal price, may be much smaller (perhaps even zero in the cases reviewed in section 4.5.3).

Another problem is that a benefactor—if known to have the intention of intervening—immediately raises the price at which lenders are willing to sell their claims. This point has been made by Dooley (1987). If, say, the donor is willing to purchase $100 million of Argentina's debt, the price at which any lender will be willing to sell can only be the post-repurchase price, which is obviously higher than the one observed ex ante on the market. (In Cohen and Verdier 1990, it is shown, however, that "secret buy-backs" are a good thing for both the creditors and the debtor.)

4.6.2 How Should a Donor Help an Indebted Country?[1]

Does that mean that lenders should renounce the idea that they can purchase the debt at its market value, that is, at the *pre-intervention* price? Assume that the donor offers lenders the following alternative deal: sell (collectively) dx units of their claims on the country at its marginal price *or* the lenders will simply make the country a gift corresponding to the market value of these dx units. The gift will be offered through an account at the Bank for International Settlements, an account that the lenders cannot seize. Let us see how the deal must be arranged to make sure that the lenders will not refuse it. Consider the case in which all lenders act in a collectively rational way, and—dropping the index 3 corresponding to the third-period outcome—define the market value of the repayment R due as in equation (14):

$$V = \frac{1}{1+r} \int_0^{R/\lambda} \lambda Q dF(Q) + \frac{1}{1+r} [1 - F(R/\lambda)]. \tag{23}$$

The donor wants to purchase dx units at the marginal price $q_m = [1 - F(R/\lambda)] [1/(1 + r)]$ [see equation (15)]. Call $dZ = q_m \cdot dx$ the value of the transfer that the benefactor is ready to make. What would be the post-deal consumption of the country if the deal were accepted? The face value of the debt would be reduced by

$$dR = \frac{1}{q_m} dZ,$$

so that the utility of the country would be increased by

$$dEV(C) = d \left\{ \int_0^{R/\lambda} u[(1 - \lambda)Q] dF(Q) + \int_{R/\lambda}^{\infty} u(Q - R) dF(Q) \right\}. \tag{24}$$

In case the lenders refuse the deal, let us now assume that the benefactor offers the country a transfer $dR = 1/q_m \cdot dZ$ whenever $Q > R/\lambda$. The expected cost for the benefactor of such a gift corresponds to the price the benefactor is willing to pay. The impact for the utility of the country, on the other hand, is obviously identical to that obtained in equation (24).

The proposed deal has the same cost for the donor and the same impact for the borrower, whether the lenders accept it or not. Only the lenders would lose if they were to reject it. They should not. A donor should be able to help an LDC without the banks grasping a part of what is intended to be a gift to the country.

4.7   Conclusion

This chapter has shown the key relevance of the distinction between the average and the marginal price of the debt. The average price of the debt reflects the value for an individual investor of an extra dollar of a country's debt; the marginal price reflects the value of this extra dollar for the community of lenders as a whole. I have shown empirically that the marginal price is likely to be very small and—in a few cases—negative.

This discrepancy between the social and the private value of a dollar of a country's debt explains why private lending to sovereign states is likely to be inefficient. It also shows why a donor that wants to help an indebted country should not try to intervene on the secondary market but rather should make a take-it-or-leave-it offer to the community of lenders. I have shown how such an offer could be made credible: the donor should threaten to give directly to the debtor the money that is offered to the creditors—if they were to refuse it.

Appendix A: The Efficient Rescheduling of Debt (proof of Proposition 1)

Let us call $[R_{12}^{(i)}, R_{13}^{(i)}]$, $i = 1, 2, 3$, the repayments that the banks ask in each of the three rescheduling schemes under study. Call $\Psi_3^{(i)}$ the "modified" probability of default such as defined in equation (19) of chapter 3. The banks' expected profits can be written

$$\pi[R_{12}^{(i)}, R_{13}^{(i)}] = R_{12}^{(i)} + \frac{1}{1+r}[1 - \Psi_3^{(i)}]R_{13}^{(i)}. \tag{A1}$$

When the country has access to the world financial markets (schemes (1) and (2)), it can borrow an amount $D_{23}^{(i)}$ and repay $R_{23}^{(i)}$. One has $D_{23}^{(i)} = (1/(1+r))[1 - \Psi_3^{(i)}]R_{23}^{(i)}$. The first-order conditions that determine $D_{23}^{(i)}$ as a function of $R_{12}^{(i)}$ and $R_{13}^{(i)}$ can be written

$$u'(C_2^{(i)})\left[1 - \Psi_3^{(i)} - R_{23}^{(i)}\frac{d\Psi_3^{(i)}}{dR^{(i)}}\right] = \beta(1+r)Eu'[C_3^{(i)}],$$

that is,

$$u'(C_2^{(i)})\left[1 - \Psi_3^{(i)} - \frac{R_{23}^{(i)}}{[R_{13}^{(i)} + R_{23}^{(i)}]}\int_0^{[R_{13}^{(i)} + R_{23}^{(i)}]/\lambda}\lambda Q_3 dF(Q_3)\right]$$

$$= \beta(1+r)Eu'[C_3^{(i)}]. \tag{A2}$$

Let us now first compare cases (1) and (3). In case (1), the banks set $R_{13}^{(i)} = 0$ and the country is free to go on the world financial markets.

The banks set $R_{12}^{(i)}$ as large as possible, subject to the constraint that $U_2(R_{12}^{(i)}, 0, Q_2) \geqslant U_a(Q_2)$. From equation (8) the first-order condition (A2) that sets the country's borrowing program can now simply be written

$$u'[C_2^{(i)}][1 - \pi_3^{(i)}] = \beta(1 + r)Eu'[C_3^{(i)}]. \tag{A3}$$

Let us now consider case (3). The banks want to maximize $R_{12}^{(3)} + (1/(1 + r))R_{13}^{(3)} [1 - \Psi_3^{(3)}]$ subject to the nonrepudiation constraint. By duality, one immediately sees that the first-order condition of the problem is as in (A3). The solution is simply

$$R_{12}^{(3)} = R_{12}^{(1)} - D_{23}^{(1)}; \qquad R_{13}^{(3)} = R_{23}^{(1)}, \tag{A4}$$

and the expected payoff is the same as in case (1).

Let us now analyze the intermediate case (2). It cannot be that the banks can get more in case (2) than in case (3). Indeed, being risk-neutral and facing the same opportunity cost as their competitive "outside" counterparts, they can always mimic in case (3) whatever outcome is reached in case (2). What we have to show is that they may lose if they were to require $R_{13}^{(2)} > 0$. This is indeed apparent from the comparison between equation (8) and equation (A2). When $R_{13}^{(i)} > 0$, the first-order condition that is solved by the country (when it goes on the financial market) tilts the balance in favor of a larger C_2: the country is induced to "overborrow." The intuition is simple: when it owes $R_{13}^{(2)} > 0$, the country is induced to take more risk than is optimal and to "dilute" among a larger number of creditors the payments that fall due when it cannot pay the debt in full (see Proposition 2 for more details).

Appendix B: The Inefficiency of Private Lending (demonstration of Proposition 2)

With respect to the initial market equilibrium, let us increase long-term debt by the amount ε and reduce the demand for short-term credit in period 2 in such a manner as to leave the risk π^* unchanged. Let us also reduce the volume of short-term debt repayment R_{12} by the amount $(1/(1 + r))E((1 - \psi_3^*))\varepsilon$. I will demonstrate that these changes strictly improve the country's position and do not reduce the banks' repayment. In period 3, the country's position is by definition unchanged, as we have kept the probability π_3^* constant. Accordingly the country's consumption remains

$$C_3 = (\text{Max } Q_3 - \lambda Q_3^*, (1 - \lambda)Q_3); \qquad \pi_3^* = F_3(Q_3^*).$$

In period 2, the country's consumption is subjected to two modifying influences. First, the volume of indebtedness D_{23} is restricted by

$$\Delta D_{23} = -\frac{1}{1 + r}\varepsilon(1 - \psi_3).$$

But, at the same time, the repayment R_{12} is reduced by

$$\Delta R_{12} = -\frac{1}{1 + r}\varepsilon E(1 - \psi_3).$$

Hence the new consumption stream in period 2 is written

$$C_{12}' = C_2 + \frac{1}{1 + r}\varepsilon[E\psi_3 - \psi_3].$$

We have therefore changed consumption C_2 by a zero-average term that is, however, countercyclical to the original value. As we have assumed that the country is not risk-neutral, the outcome is an improvement in its utility—provided ε is sufficiently small. Also, when $Q_2 = Q_2^*$, the country's utility is strictly greater than the initial level. The country will no longer choose to default on the initial value, but on a lower one. In other words, debt D_1 will be more than repaid by the change

$$\Delta R_{13} = \varepsilon$$

$$\Delta R_{23} = -\varepsilon\frac{1}{1 + r}E(1 - \psi_3).$$

In short, the new program is feasible and strictly dominates the one obtained through market equilibrium. This proves my proposition.

III | HOW TO EVALUATE THE SOLVENCY OF AN INDEBTED NATION

When the IMF or the World Bank designs the stabilization program of an indebted nation, which current account should they target for the country? Should the program be designed with a view to servicing all interest falling due? What is the benchmark for a country to be declared solvent? In this part of the book I distinguish three criteria. The first is directly derived from the standard finance literature and draws on the analysis presented in chapter 1. The value of an asset is the sum of the discounted values of all the dividends attached to it. Applied to the debt of a nation, this criterion is expressed as follows: the value of a debt is equal to the present discounted value of all future debt service. The service of the debt may be spread out intertemporally, but in all events the income flows transferred from the debtor nation to its creditors must add up to the face value of the debt (when one rules out the case in which lenders behave inefficiently, as shown in chapter 2). This criterion was derived in part I, when the threat of debt repudiation was not taken into account.

The second criterion that a stabilization program must satisfy is the following: the intertemporal pattern of current accounts designed by the IMF or the World Bank must be politically feasible at all points in time, not only at the outset. The program must never induce the country to repudiate its debt either initially or at some later time. This second constraint may be called the nonrepudiation constraint and draws on the analysis outlined in part II.

It is clear that these two criteria impose two different constraints. A program that postpones the burden of servicing the debt may satisfy, in principle, the first criterion; yet the implementation of the tough part of the program may induce the country to renege on its earlier commitments. On the other hand, a loose program may be feasible, but only at the cost of failing to generate enough transfer of income from the debtor to its creditors.

A third criterion, however, must be applied to a stabilization program: namely, the solvency constraint of the *government*, which must be carefully distinguished from that of the country. A country may achieve a trade surplus (say, through a sharp cut in its imports), but this is not the end of the story. If the external debt is a government debt (as it mostly is in the case of LDCs), then the government must raise the resources it needs to finance it. Otherwise, domestic debt will be substituted for the external debt, and the stabilization program may collapse along with the country's domestic financial market. This will be shown in chapter 7.

In this part of the book, I spell out the arithmetic and the empirical implications of these criteria. I show that most indebted nations need to allocate only 15% of their exports to meet the first two of the above criteria. However, I also indicate that a country like Brazil, while passing this test, failed to meet the third criterion. The service of its external debt was accompanied by an 80% rise in its domestic debt. I conclude that Brazil should have slowed down the service of its external debt and increased the service of its domestic debt.

Let us now examine the implications of each of these three criteria in greater detail.

Criterion 1:   The Solvency Constraint

According to this criterion, the discounted sum of all resource balances must add up to the initial face value of the debt. The discount factor here is the real world rate of interest paid on the debt. Consider, for instance, the case of a country whose resource balance always exactly matches the interest falling due. Every period, all of the principal is refinanced, and thus the outstanding debt of the country stays constant. It is an easy accounting exercise to check that the country is solvent according to the first criterion (when interest rates are positive). How can it be checked in the case of more sophisticated stabilization programs? Do we need to rely on a case-by-case analysis? Fortunately, the answer to this latter question is negative; there is a simple way of assessing whether the first criterion is satisfied or not. It is the "transversality condition" that was obtained in chapter 2.

This condition says that the face value of the debt will be equal to the sum of the discounted values of the resource balances of the country *if and only if,* at the limit, the discounted value of the debt tends to zero. In order to meet the first criterion, a country must bring the value of its outstanding debt down to zero *when the debt is measured in discounted terms.* On this criterion it is clear that a country that services all interest falling due meets the first criterion when interest rates are strictly positive. Indeed, the country's debt stays constant, so that its discounted value tends to zero.

This seemingly innocuous result has in fact very important implications. Consider a world financial market in which real interest rates are positive and a country that *always* services *half* of the interest falling due and refinances both the principal and the remainder of the interest. Is such a

country solvent according to the first criterion? The answer is unambiguously affirmative, as the transversality condition reveals. Indeed, though
the country's debt is continually increasing, its growth rate is "only" half
the interest rate. Since the discount factor is one over one plus the interest
rate itself, a little knowledge of algebra suffices to check that the discounted
value of the debt does indeed tend to zero. More generally, if the outstanding value of the debt displays a positive growth rate that is strictly
lower than the interest rate, clearly the same finding will hold: the country
does indeed meet the first criterion. The intuition behind this finding may
be expressed as follows. Take again the case of a country servicing half of
the interest falling due. Even though this effort does not seem as great as
that of servicing all of the interest falling due, it is an effort that is growing
at exactly half of the pace of the interest rate itself. The nation pays half of
a term that is growing twice as fast. Let us take another extreme case. If
the country was regularly repaying one-tenth of the interest falling due, the
rate of growth of the outstanding debt would be nine-tenths of the interest
rate, so that once again the transversality condition would be satisfied, but
the country's effort to service its debt would rapidly increase, as would the
outstanding debt itself.

Criterion 2:   The Nonrepudiation Constraint

This extreme example illuminates the need to check the second criterion.
It is not enough for a stabilization program to reschedule the debt on the
first criterion alone. It must also be checked that the program is politically
feasible in the long run. If it is targeted, for instance, that all GDP must be
absorbed to service the debt, the underlying program has little chance of
being adopted in the real world. At some point the country will undoubtedly choose to repudiate its debt rather than starve.

There is one obvious benchmark against which one can check the feasibility of a program: it is that the growth rate of the debt is no greater than
that of the country's resources. Should the debt-to-export—or the debt-to-
GDP—ratio steadily decline, then a program that is willingly implemented
at some initial time should also be willingly followed later on. In the
meantime, indeed, the debt will have shrunk as a proportion of the country's resources. In chapter 5 I spell out a framework of analysis in which
this intuition is exactly right. Specifically, I first calculate the minimum

percentage of a country's resources that must be transferred to its creditors in order to satisfy criterion 1. I then show that a country that has willingly agreed to service that percentage should be expected to do the same later on. Call *b* this percentage.

b is an index that depends both on the current value of the debt-to-earnings (debt-to-exports or debt-to-GDP) ratio and on *expected* future growth and interest rates. It is therefore, I believe, a better financial indicator than the static ones (debt-to-exports, debt-to-GDP, or the debt-service ratio) that are customarily used. Indeed, it makes little sense to contend, for instance, that a debt-to-export ratio of 3 is high or low per se. It may be low for a country whose growth prospects are considerable and high for a declining country; my index *b* explicitly embodies these features. It will be low for countries with high growth or low interest rates and high otherwise.

In chapter 6 I show that *b* (almost) never exceeds 15% of the value of a country's exports. To ascertain the intuition underlying this result, let us assume that the debt-to-export ratio of a nation is 3 and that the difference between real world interest rates and the country's rate of growth is constant and always equal to 5%. In this case, the value of *b* is 15% ($=3 \times 5\%$): any resource surplus marginally greater than 15% would bring down the debt-to-export ratio. Therefore, if such a country is willing to attain such a trade surplus today, it will certainly be willing to do it later, since its debt-to-export ratio will have gone down. There, in this case, 15% of a country's exports is sufficient to satisfy both the solvency and the feasibility constraints.

To illustrate these results, let us take the case of Brazil. From 1983 to 1985, Brazil's debt service has represented, on average, 30% of its exports. It is twice as much as suggested by my index. As a result, the net debt-to-export ratio has been brought down very substantially, from a peak of 4 in 1982 to 3 at the end of 1986. On the basis of the foregoing I would argue that this fall is too rapid and that it could usefully be slowed down. Consider, in this light, Brazil's proposal to limit the service of its debt to 2.5% of GDP. Brazil's external debt-to-GDP ratio is 40%. If one takes, as a benchmark, the pessimistic assumption that the difference between world interest rates and the growth rate of Brazil's GDP is 5%, it will be seen that it takes 2% of GDP to stabilize the debt-to-GDP ratio. Brazil's suggestion that its debt service equal 2.5% of its GDP is therefore perfectly reasonable.

Criterion 3: The Government Budget Constraint

The external debt of LDCs is primarily government debt. When a country achieves a resource surplus, it is necessary to know if this external surplus derives from a primary domestic government. If it does not, two things (and two things only) can happen: 1. the government monetizes its resource surplus (i.e., it sells cruzeiros, or cruzados, to buy the dollars earned by its exporters); 2. it increases its domestic debt to finance the purchase of the exporters' dollars. Both processes have an upper limit. Monetizing the surplus triggers inflation. This is bad, but so long as it channels resources to the government, this may be the only option open: increasing the seigniorage tax is a sure way to raise the government's income. Yet it is well known in monetary theory that the seigniorage tax has an upper bound in real terms: there is a maximum inflation rate above which more money creation *reduces* the government's real income. It is the point at which any increase in the inflation rate reduces private sector money demand by more than the inflation rate itself. As a result, beyond that point, the government cannot increase its real income by printing money. There is plenty of evidence that Brazil reached the point in December 1985. Money creation could no longer increase government income.

The second option for the government is to increase its domestic debt in order to service its external debt. The limit to this process is the limitations of domestic financial markets. In 1985, Brazil's domestic real rate of interest reached the extraordinary level of 20%. At this rate, compounded (domestic) interest rates swiftly dictate policy. These issues are discussed in chapter 7.

5 A Solvency Index: Theory

In the previous parts, we have seen that the threat of debt repudiation changed the functioning of the financial markets in many qualitatively fundamental ways. In this part, I want to address the quantitative aspect of the problem. How should one empirically assess whether or not indebted nations have passed the point at which they would rather repudiate their debt than service it in full?

To attack this problem, I will first cast the issue of debt repudiation in the framework of a simple infinitely lived deterministic exchange economy. I will leave aside two key features of the scenario: that of dealing with the domestic tax problem faced by the government and that of dealing with risk and endogenous growth; these are the topics of chapter 7 and of part IV, respectively.

In this chapter I attempt to show that a simple criterion may go a long way toward revealing whether or not, ceteris paribus, a country is "solvent," that is, whether or not a country would prefer servicing its debt in full to defaulting, one day or another. This criterion will measure the *fixed share* of a country's resources (defined in this chapter) that a country should allocate to repay its external debt. Here "repay" means that the sum of transfers made abroad (appropriately measured in discounted terms) exactly matches the net external indebtedness of the country. With this definition, a country that can credibly commit itself to generate such a sequence of trade balance surpluses over the infinite future must be defined as solvent. How can one check whether or not the promise to generate such a sequence of trade surpluses is credible? Within the framework presented in this chapter, I show that a country that chooses to start implementing a stabilization program aimed at reaching the trade criterion defined above is indeed solvent and may be trusted to implement the same program later on. Generating a trade balance surplus greater than my proposed criterion simply amounts to stabilizing, on average, the debt-to-GDP ratio. If a country agrees to start implementing a program to stabilize the debt-to-GDP ratio, its reasons (whatever they may be) will induce it to do the same later on. This is essentially what this chapter aims to prove.

One immediate consequence of this solvency criterion is that a country that is infinitely wealthy (whose present value of its resources is infinite) will always be solvent. This should come as no surprise and is a direct application of the discussion in section 2.2. For the reasons stated in chapter 2, we shall disregard that case and assume that the wealth of the nation is finite. Yet the extreme case in which wealth is infinite (and in which the fraction of its resources that the country should transfer to its creditor shrinks to zero) may be interpreted as a meaningful case, that in which the debt can be indefinitely rescheduled in the manner suggested by the overlapping generations model.

5.1   A Framework of Analysis

I will now extend, in a simple infinitely lived deterministic exchange economy, the framework examined in part II. For the reasons spelled out in chapter 2, I will assume that the wealth of the nation is finite. This will imply, in particular, that growth rates will not be systematically larger than interest rates. The criterion that I spell out below shows that the magnitude of the difference between the two rates (and not only its sign) will play, as it is intuitive, a crucial role in the investigation of the country's solvency.

5.1.1   An Infinitely Lived Exchange Economy

Let us first consider an infinitely lived economy whose resources are unambiguously measured by an exogenous endowment $(Q_t)_{t \geqslant 1}$ in the only good that, I assume, is consumed and traded in the world. In section 5.4, I extend the analysis to the case in which two goods (a traded one and a nontraded one) are produced and exchanged and show how one should appropriately measure the wealth of the country.

Call r_t the world rate of interest and D_t the outstanding debt of the country at the end of time t. Following chapter 1's convention, we can write the law of motion of the country's debt as

$$D_t = (1 + r_t)D_{t-1} + C_t - Q_t.$$

At initial time $t = 0$, the country is assumed to start with no initial debt so that, whatever the choices made by the country, the sequence $(C_t)_{t \geqslant 0}$ will necessarily have to be subject to the intertemporal budget constraint:

$$\sum_{t=0}^{\infty} \frac{C_t}{\prod_{s=0}^{t} (1 + r_s)} = \sum_{t=0}^{\infty} \frac{Q_t}{\prod_{s=0}^{t} (1 + r_s)} \equiv W. \tag{1}$$

W is the initial wealth that the country chooses to spend over time, which will be assumed to be finite for the reasons spelled out in chapter 2. As also shown in chapter 2, this equality is equivalent to the transversality condition:

$$\lim_{t \to \infty} \frac{D_t}{\prod_{s=0}^{t} (1 + r_s)} = 0. \tag{2}$$

Now, contrary to the cases examined in chapter 1, the country is not free to choose *any* pattern C_t that lies along the budget constraint (1). Because of the threat of debt repudiation, lenders want to make sure that the debt is never so big as to make the country prefer defaulting to servicing it.

5.1.2   The Threat of Debt Repudiation

Let us assume that the threat of debt repudiation works in the same manner as in the previous chapter. At any point in time, a country that has defaulted on its debt will be subject to the following sanctions:

1) It will suffer a loss of output equal to a proportion λ of its GDP forever after it has defaulted.

2) It will be forced to maintain financial autarky forever after it has defaulted. This means that it can never borrow or lend (or keep reserves) from the time it has defaulted onward.

Both sanctions may appear too harsh with respect to what historical precedent reveals. A country is never barred forever after it has defaulted. Instead, after some time, a defaulting country always resumes participation in the financial markets. At the same time, however, the country may always keep some reserves (gold, for instance) that lenders cannot seize. However, none of these remarks are really crucial. What really matters is that credible sanctions are available to the lenders. Otherwise, as we shall see, no credit could ever be offered. Assumptions 1 and 2 have the advantage of making the analysis much more tractable. Indeed, they will impose that the consumption path of a defaulting country is perfectly known to be

$$C_t^d = (1 - \lambda)Q_t. \tag{3}$$

On the one hand, financial autarky imposes that the country consumes exactly whatever resources it may have (no intertemporal smoothing is allowed after default). On the other hand, the cost of debt repudiation scales down GDP by a factor λ.

5.1.3   The Country's Intertemporal Objective

Leaving aside the issues of domestic taxation and domestic conflict of interest, I will simply assume that the country is managed by a social planner whose objective is to maximize the following criterion:

$$U = \sum_{t=0}^{\infty} \beta^t u(C_t), \tag{4}$$

in which u is a utility function that satisfies

$$\lim_{x \to 0} u'(x) = \infty.$$

Futhermore, in all that follows I will assume that β is low enough to guarantee that the country is a net debtor in the long run.

5.2   Equilibrium in the Credit Market

5.2.1   When the Threat of Debt Repudiation Is Not Credible ($\lambda = 1$)

Let us first examine the outcome of the country's borrowing strategy in the extreme case in which the country has in fact no option of repudiating its debt, because lenders' sanctions would wipe out all of its GDP. In that case, the credit markets perform efficiently along the lines spelled out in chapter 1. The only constraint the country must obey is the intertemporal equality between spending and resources. Call λ_0 the Lagrange multiplier associated with this constraint. The country's optimal consumption path is a solution to

$$\beta^t u'(C_t) = \lambda_0 \frac{1}{\displaystyle\prod_{s=0}^{t}(1 + r_s)}, \tag{5}$$

that is,

$$u'(C_t) = \left[\beta^t \prod_{s=0}^{t}(1 + r_s) \right]^{-1} \cdot \lambda_0. \tag{6}$$

The equilibrium value of λ_0 is obtained by requiring that the sequence C_t obeys the intertemporal budget constraint (1). Whatever this value may be, let us assume now that β is low enough that

$$\lim_{t \to \infty} \beta^t \prod_{s=0}^{t}(1 + r_s) = 0.$$

(If, in the long run, the interest rate converges toward a value r, this amounts to imposing that $\beta(1 + r) < 1$.) In that case, equation (6) shows that consumption in the country would converge toward zero asymptotically. As time passes, this means that the country's indebtedness becomes so heavy that the service of the debt absorbs gradually all of the country's GDP: The country's initial borrowing strategy pushes its long-run equilibrium consumption path toward asymptotic starvation.

The low discount factor explains why the country is willing to trade more initial consumption against long-run asymptotic starvation. While optimal initially, it is a choice that, in the long run, the country will wish it had never made. Yet, if no capacity for repudiating the debt is available, the country will have no choice but to fulfill its initial commitments. On the other hand, if any option of repudiating the debt is available, however costly it may be, it will certainly be exercised. It is in view of this threat of debt repudiation, if it exists, that the lender will ration the country's demand of credit.

5.2.2 Lending Strategy under Threat of Debt Repudiation

What then should be the credit ceiling that lenders must impose on borrowers in order to avoid default? To answer this question, let us first define a "tight" credit ceiling as one that cannot be relaxed without inducing a country to default.

DEFINITION 1:   One credit ceiling is strictly "looser" than another if it never induces a country to borrow less and if, at least once, it induces the country to borrow more. A "tight" credit ceiling is one that can never be "loosened" without inducing the country to default.

In order to characterize the "tight" credit ceiling that the lenders will want to adopt, let us first prove:

PROPOSITION 1:   On any interval during which the country has reached the limit imposed by a "tight" credit ceiling, the country will never be willing to pay its creditors more than the cost of debt repudiation (λQ_t).

In other words, consider an interval of time $[t, t + T]$ $(T \geqslant 1)$ during which the country has reached its upper limit of debt. Proposition 1 says that at no point $s \in [t, t + T]$ will the country be willing to pay its creditors more than λQ.

Proof of Proposition 1:   If the country has reached a tight credit ceiling constraint, this must imply that, in that interval $[t, t + T]$, the utility provided by abiding by the constraint and the utility that would be obtained by defaulting are identical from the country's viewpoint. We must therefore have

$\forall s \in [t, t + T]$:

$$\sum_{j=s}^{\infty} \beta^{j-s} u[Q_t - \bar{P}_t] = \sum_{j=s}^{\infty} \beta^{j-s} u[Q_t(1 - \lambda)], \tag{7}$$

in which $\bar{P}_t$ is the payment necessary to abide by the credit ceiling, that is,

$$\bar{P}_t = \bar{D}_t - (1 + r_t)\bar{D}_{t-1}.$$

Assume that $T > 1$, then subtracting equation (7) (when written) for $s = t$ from its value (when written) for $s = t + 1$ (and multiplying by β), one sees that

$$u(Q_t - \bar{P}_t) = u[Q_t(1 - \lambda)],$$

therefore

$$\bar{P}_t = \lambda Q_t. \quad \text{Q.E.D.}$$

An important implication of Proposition 1 is the following corollary.

Corollary: The threat of financial autarky is never sufficient to keep a country from defaulting.

Indeed, consider the case when $\lambda = 0$; the lenders, then, can only threaten a defaulting country with the prospect of financial autarky. One sees from Proposition 1 that a country can never then be kept from defaulting, if any positive amount of debt is asked for repayment. The results that obviously held in the finitely lived economy also hold here, in the infinite horizon case. (See Bulow and Rogoff 1989b for another framework in which this result is obtained.)

One can now readily find the credit ceiling that the banks should impose. On the one hand, the country will never want to pay more than λQ_t when the credit ceiling binds. On the other hand, paying λQ_t all the time is not worse than defaulting, so that the banks can safely set the following "tight" credit ceiling:

$$\bar{D}_t = \sum_{s=1}^{\infty} \frac{\lambda Q_{t+s}}{\prod_{j=t+1}^{t+s} (1 + r_j)}.$$

Define

$$W_t \equiv \sum_{s=1}^{\infty} \frac{Q_{t+s}}{\prod_{j=t+1}^{t+s} (1 + r_j)}$$

as the present value of the country's future resources. The credit ceiling may simply be characterized by the inequality

$$D_t \leqslant \lambda W_t. \tag{8}$$

Lenders should never let the country borrow more than a fraction of its wealth. That fraction, in the model presented here, is nothing but the cost of debt repudiation itself.

We shall say that a country that satisfies (8) is "solvent." Lenders can indeed impose a credible repayment path $P_t = \lambda Q_t$, which is sufficient to repay the debt and on which the country will never want to default. In the case when $\lambda = 1$, lenders should only be concerned with restraining the country's debt from exceeding its wealth.

5.3   An Index of Solvency

5.3.1   Definition

Based on the results obtained in the previous section, let us now see how one could rely upon a simple index of solvency to assess whether a country would repudiate its debt rather that service it in full. If the lenders (or economists) were to know precisely the cost of debt repudiation, there would be no problem. A natural index of solvency would be

$$a = \frac{D_t}{\lambda W_t}.$$

Any index $a \leqslant 1$ would reveal a solvent country, and any index $a > 1$ would reveal that the country will never want to repay its debt in full.

Let us assume instead that lenders do not know the value of λ with accuracy. They have lent D_t to a country, and they wonder whether the country is solvent or not. This is the kind of problem that arose in 1982. Due to a change of environment, lenders were taken by surprise by Mexico's decision to suspend debt service. Taking as a given the new economic environment of the 1980s, their question at the time was: Is Mexico solvent? In other words, is Mexico ready to embark upon a stabilization program that will service the debt in full?

To help answer this question, let us define an index of solvency b as

$$b \equiv \frac{D_t}{W_t}, \tag{9}$$

where b is the ratio of the country's outstanding debt to its wealth. To calculate b, one needs to know the debt of the country (which is no problem in theory but may involve some technical problems in practice; see chapter 6), and the wealth W_t of the country defined as

$$W_t \equiv \sum_{s=1}^{\infty} \frac{Q_{t+s}}{\prod_{j=t+1}^{t+s} (1 + r_j)},$$

which, in order to be measured, requires the ability to foresee the available growth and interest rates. (For the case in which growth is endogenous, see chapter 8.) In practice, in the next chapter, I will make reasonably pessimistic assumptions to be on the safe side of b's estimate.

5.3.2 Intuition

A simple way to understand the economic content of b is to write (9) as a solution to

$$D_t = \sum_{s=1}^{\infty} \frac{bQ_{t+s}}{\prod_{j=t+1}^{t+s} (1 + r_j)}. \tag{10}$$

With this equation, b is simply that fixed fraction of the country's resources that has to be allocated to the service of the debt. The service of the debt is designed to make sure that the sum of the transfers that are henceforth generated exactly matches the face value of the country's outstanding debt. In the simple case when growth and interest rates are constant ($r_t = r, n_t = n, \forall t$), this equation is turned into

$$b = (r - n)\frac{D_t}{Q_{t+1}}. \tag{11}$$

The index b, here, is simply proportional to the debt-to-GDP ratio and to the difference between growth and interest rates. In this case, paying bQ_t is needed to stabilize the debt-to-GDP ratio. Indeed, the law of motion of the debt is

$$D_{t+1} = (1 + r)D_t - bQ_{t+1}, \tag{12}$$

that is,

$$D_{t+1} = (1 + r)D_t - (r - n)D_t$$
$$= (1 + n)D_t. \tag{13}$$

The debt has the same growth rate as GDP, so that the debt-to-GDP ratio is stabilized. We know already, from the definition of b, that such a strategy amounts to transferring the face value of the debt to the lenders. In the specific case when growth and interest rates are constant, there is an easy way to check this property. When the debt grows at a rate $n < r$, it is indeed straightforward to check that the transversality condition

$$\lim_{t \to \infty} \frac{D_t}{(1 + r)^t} = 0$$

(which was shown in chapter 2 to be equivalent to the solvency condition) is necessarily satisfied.

In the limiting case when $n = r$, $b = 0$, so the borrowers are required to pay nothing. This limiting case is no puzzle: it corresponds exactly to the case examined in chapter 2. The wealth of the nation is infinite, and it takes no resources to stabilize the debt-to-GDP ratio: one simply needs to reschedule the debt in a never-ending way. The main lesson of chapter 2 was precisely that such an idyllic state of affairs could not be expected to last forever (even though it may continue for a long time). Yet it is important that an index of solvency should declare a country perfectly solvent *were* this state of affairs to occur.

5.3.3 Properties of the b-statistic

If λ were known to the lenders, they could asses whether or not a country is solvent simply by comparing b to λ. If $b > \lambda$, the borrower will never agree to repay its debt in full; conversely, if $b < \lambda$, then the country would not have yet exhausted its credit ceiling. When $b = \lambda$, the lenders' strategy is simple: they should simply ask the country to pay bQ_t all the time.

Let us now investigate what happens when λ is not accurately known. More specifically, let us assume that the lenders have an idea $\hat{\lambda}$ of λ, which need not be the correct one but which the lenders themselves do not doubt. Let us assume that at some time—say 1982—the lenders believed that $b = \hat{\lambda}$: they thought that the country had exhausted its credit ceiling and, according to Proposition 1, they asked the country to generate a trade surplus $TB_{t_0} = bQ_{t_0}$. What happens then?

PROPOSITION 2: If a country that is believed to have reached its credit ceiling at some time agrees to generate a trade surplus $TB_{t_0} = bQ_{t_0}$, then the country is necessarily solvent and it will also agree, at a later time $t \geq t_0$, to pay $TB_t = bQ_t$. On the other hand, if the country would rather default than pay bQ_{t_0}, then it is necessarily insolvent.

In other words, in the wake of the 1982 crisis, when most countries were precipitously asked to pay lenders their due, one can argue that those countries that did manage to reach a trade-to-GDP ratio above b were solvent. To repeat: *it is not necessary to know λ, the cost of debt repudiation, to make this diagnosis.*

The proof of this proposition is straightforward. If the country prefers to stabilize its debt-to-wealth ratio today—rather than defaulting—it will be willing to do the same in the future as well. If it does prefer defaulting to stabilizing its debt-to-wealth ratio, it must mean that it cannot service its debt in full (and postponing the service of the debt will not help).

5.4 The Definition of a Country's Resources: An "Invariant" Measure of Wealth

5.4.1 Definition

Up to now we have supposed that a country's wealth could be measured by its endowments in a single good. I would like, in this section, to set up an analytical framework allowing us to approach the problem of defining a country's wealth when the country produces several goods.

Suppose the country produces two goods: a home good (that is not traded internationally) and an export good. To simplify, we assume that national residents consume only the domestic good but that, in order to produce it, they need an imported input. Call sector 1 the home goods sector and sector 2 the exported goods sector. We suppose that the production technology in each of these sectors is

$$\begin{cases} Q_1 = M_1^{1-\alpha}\Omega_1^{\alpha} \\ Q_2 = \Omega_2; \quad \Omega_1 + \Omega_2 \leqslant \bar{\Omega}, \end{cases} \tag{12}$$

where $\bar{\Omega}$ measures the country's resources in a good (capital, or human capital) that is not directly observable. We take imports as numeraire. Call p_2 the terms of trade (the relative price of exports); this gives

$$M = p_2 Q_2 - P,$$

where P measures the trade surplus. We suppose that the penalty λ resulting from debt repudiation applies to exports (which may be partly confiscated by creditors). A country that elects to repudiate its debt in period t can thus only import

$$M_{t+s} = p_2(1 - \lambda)Q_{2,t+s}$$

(if it produces a quantity $Q_{2,t+s}$ of exportable goods). Take the world interest rates to be constant and let $U(D, \Omega)$ be the utility that the country would get by not defaulting on its debt, and $U_d(\Omega)$ the utility it would get by defaulting. In this new analytical framework, the creditors' strategy must always be defined such that $U(D, \Omega) \geqslant U_d(\Omega)$ and, as before, the model's linearity ensures that this inequality also gives $U(zD, z\Omega) \geqslant U_d(z\Omega)$. As before, creditors' optimal strategy will take the form

$$\frac{D_t}{\Omega_t} \leqslant h_t^*. \tag{13}$$

The new problem that must now be resolved is the following: how to define (13) when creditors observe only exports and GDP (and not resources Ω)? In other words, what is the best "proxy" for the country's resources Ω: export volumes, GDP, or some other intermediary measure?

To resolve this problem, we will start by supposing that the (domestic) prices in force are Walrasian prices. In this case

$$p_1 = \frac{1}{\alpha^{\alpha}(1 - \alpha)^{1-\alpha}} p_2^{\alpha};$$

GDP $(= p_1 Q_1 + p_2 Q_2 - M)$ is then simply written

$$\text{GDP} = p_2\bar{\Omega},$$

and exports

$$X = p_2(1 - \alpha)\bar{\Omega} + \alpha P.$$

We thus see in this case that GDP is a direct measure of resources Ω, and exports an indirect one.

However, creditors are faced with the following "moral hazard" problem. If they decide to base their lending policy on the GDP measure, they will encourage the debtor country to change its relative price structure in such a way as to increase artificially the value of its GDP (by overvaluing its currency). Conversely, if lenders base their calculations on the export measure, they will induce the country to change its policy in the opposite direction: the country will devalue its currency inefficiently. Thus, both measures create a distortion, but with opposite signs. This enables us to define an invariant measure of wealth.

Suppose that the country decides to ration its imports or subsidize its exports to distort the relative price structure. Let γ be the resultant shadow price of imports. When $\gamma = 1$, the price of imports is the world price. When $\gamma > 1$, imports are rationed and their shadow price (given by the black market) is higher than the world price. When $\gamma < 1$, exports are subsidized and their shadow price is above the world market price. With this measure γ of the price distortion, we find that GDP and exports become

$$\begin{cases} \text{GDP} = \dfrac{1}{1 + \alpha(\gamma - 1)}[\gamma p_2\bar{\Omega} - (1 - \alpha)(\gamma - 1)P] \\[2mm] X = \dfrac{1}{1 + \alpha(\gamma - 1)}[(1 - \alpha)p_2\bar{\Omega} + \alpha\gamma P]. \end{cases} \tag{14}$$

GDP increases with γ; by rationing imports, the country overvalues its currency and artificially inflates the GDP measure. On the other hand, exports decrease with γ, for the symmetrical reason that the currency is undervalued and the volume of exports artificially boosted.

Now let us consider the following measure:

$$Z = \frac{\alpha}{1 + \alpha}\text{GDP} + \frac{1}{1 + \alpha}X.$$

We check that Z is independent of γ. By basing their loans on Z, lenders do not induce the country to take distortionary action (and Z is linearly correlated with Ω). In short, Z does indeed provide an invariant measure of the wealth of a nation.

Because of the various assumptions we have made (notably that production is Cobb-Douglas), it is extremely easy to define W. We can extend our analysis to the more complex case where the transfer of resources from one sector to another is written

$$\Omega_1 + \theta\left(\frac{\Omega_2}{\Omega_1}\right)\Omega_2 \leqslant \bar{\Omega},$$

where θ is a decreasing function. θ may be interpreted as the cost of transferring resources from sector 1 to sector 2. This hypothesis retains the linearities we will need to write the creditors' strategy in form (13). In this new case, the definition of W should be changed as follows: α is changed into α/ϱ in equation (13) when $\varrho(\geqslant 1)$ measures the curvature of the production possibility frontier. In the extreme case where $\varrho = \infty$, no substitution is possible between the sectors, and exports define the invariant measure required by creditors to appraise their credit policies.

5.4.2   A Numerical Application

We sought an invariant wealth measure for the case of Brazil. To do so, we looked for a number k such that

$$Z = k\,\mathrm{GDP} + (1 - k)X$$

is a measure that does not depend on the real exchange rate.
    We found the following regressions:

$$\mathrm{Log}\,X(t) = 5.75 + 0.08\,\text{time} + 0.88\,\mathrm{Log}\,z(t - 1)$$
$$\qquad\quad (4.6)\quad (11.9)\qquad\quad (2.6)$$

$R^2 = 0.97 \qquad DW = 1.3$ (t-statistic in brackets)

where $z(t - 1)$ is the real exchange rate at time $t - 1$, and $X(t)$ the value of exports in constant dollars. We find a significant export response to relative prices (elasticity is 0.88). Moreover, the constant dollar value of GDP gives rise to the following regression:

$$\mathrm{Log}\,\mathrm{GDP}(t) = 14.6 + 0.06\,\text{time} - 0.78\,\mathrm{Log}\,z(t - 1)$$
$$\qquad\qquad\quad (11.5)\qquad\qquad (2.3)$$

$R^2 = 0.93 \qquad DW = 0.97$

    As expected, the real exchange rate and GDP are negatively correlated.

We looked for a value k such that $\text{Log}\,Z_t = \text{Log}[k\,\text{GDP}_t + (1 - k)X_t]$ does not depend on $z(t - 1)$. We found that the sign of the dependence of $\text{Log}\,W_t$ on $\text{Log}\,z(t - 1)$ changes for k between 0.095 and 0.1. We can thus retain

$$Z(t) = 0.1\,\text{GDP}(t) + 0.9\,X(t)$$

as Brazil's "invariant wealth measure." Because exports account for around 10% of GDP, this measure assigns the same weight to changes in GDP and changes in exports. (See van Wijnbergen et al. 1988 for an application of this technique to the case of Turkey.)

6 An Empirical Evaluation of the Solvency Index

This chapter presents an empirical estimate of the solvency index proposed in the previous chapter. The index is a measure of the share of resources that a country should transfer to its creditors in order to be declared solvent. The key point of the index is that it weights the debt-to-GDP or the debt-to-export ratio (depending on which of GDP or exports is best suited to measure the resources) by an average measure of the difference between expected growth and interest rates. A country with a large debt and fast growth may very well be more solvent that a country with a smaller debt and no growth prospects. This dynamic vision of solvency is typically omitted by all static measures such as debt-service ratios or any other debt-related aggregate. In particular, a static measure such as the debt-to-GDP ratio will systematically fail to identify that any period of time during which interest rates are lower than growth rates must weight down the burden of the debt. The index that is proposed instead explicitly takes account of this possibility.

I calculate the index in the way "well-educated" creditors could have done it at the onset of the crisis in 1982. I then compare its value to the adjustment that was actually undertaken by debtors in the 1980s. Roughly speaking, the index shows that most debtors should have paid no more than 15% of the value of their exports to be declared solvent in the 1980s. This may look like a small number. Yet one should be careful to recall how difficult it sometimes is for an industrialized country to bring its trade deficit back to balance before deciding that the number is low.

The arithmetic behind this estimate is in fact extremely simple. Taking the pessimistic view that the difference between growth and interest rates is not likely to exceed 5%, and taking a country whose debt-to-export ratio is 3, one finds that 15% of this country's exports must be paid to the country's creditors to stabilize, on average, the debt-to-export ratio.

Comparing this criterion to what actually happened during the 1980s, we shall find that many important debtors, such as Brazil or Mexico, did meet this criterion pretty well. How is it, then, that by the end of the decade both countries' debt was heavily discounted on the secondary market? This question will be addressed in the next chapter. At any rate, the calculations presented in this chapter show that it is *not* the capability (or the willingness) of these countries to reach an appropriate *trade balance* surplus that is at fault.

6.1 Hypotheses about the Calculation of the Index

The index is calculated for all countries reporting to the World Bank Debt Reporting System. To calculate the index, one needs to estimate the country's wealth and measure appropriately the country's debt.

In the last section of the previous chapter, I indicated that neither GDP nor exports is a good measure of a country's resources. One should take instead an invariant measure that is insensitive to the real exchange rate. Unfortunately, this task is far too vast to be applied to all debtor nations. For the purpose of homogeneity, I have chosen to proxy the countries' resources by the countries' exports. Exports, indeed, are a more reliable figure than GDP which, it must be stressed, would have to be converted (somewhat arbitrarily) to dollars in order to be homogeneous to the debt. In the empirical estimate, exports are chosen to be inclusive of workers' remittances from abroad.

With this convention concerning the country's resources, the solvency index b, measured at some initial time 0, is a solution to

$$D_0 = \sum_{t=1}^{\infty} \frac{bX_t}{\prod_{s=1}^{t} (1 + r_s)}, \tag{1}$$

in which X_t is the country's exports at time t.

Letting $n_t \equiv X_t/X_{t-1} - 1$ be the exports' growth rate, one can write (1) as

$$b = \left[\sum_{t=1}^{\infty} \frac{\prod_{s=1}^{t} (1 + n_s)}{\prod_{s=1}^{t} (1 + r_s)} \right]^{-1} D_0/X_0. \tag{2}$$

Equation (2) is the practical definition of b that we shall use. We shall take December 1982 as the initial time at which the calculations are made. To compute b, one now needs to make hypotheses on *future* growth and interest rates and to measure appropriately the debt-to-export ratio.

6.1.1 Hypotheses on Growth and Interest Rates

I have split the expectations on the path of growth and interest rates (such as they could be foreseen in 1982) into two components.

(1) The expectation (made in December 1982) of the years 1983–1995; (2) the expectations made over the infinite future after 1995. Specifically, these assumptions are as follows:

i) *Up to 1995*

a) *Growth rates*: We took the World Bank forecasts and *reduced* them by 1.5% per year.

b) *Interest rates*: The rates adopted up to 1996 are given below. Interest rates include bank margins and commissions.

Real interest rates to 1995

1983–1985	1986–1995
10%	7%

ii) *After 1996*

We assumed that interest rates and growth rates after 1996 will, on average, give a value corresponding to a steady state where rates r and n are constant.

In other words, we supposed that

$$b_{96} \equiv \sum_{t=96}^{\infty} \frac{\prod_{i=96}^{t} (1 + n_i)}{\prod_{i=96}^{t} (1 + r_i)} = \sum_{0}^{\infty} \frac{(1 + n)^t}{(1 + r)^t} = \frac{r - n}{1 + n} \equiv \theta_{96}. \tag{3}$$

Sticking to our strategy of taking pessimistic values, we choose a value $\theta_{96} = 5\%$: a permanent differential of 5% between growth rates and real interest rates. With this decomposition, the value of b may be written

$$b = \frac{1}{\lambda_{96} + \frac{z_{96}}{\theta_{96}}} \frac{D_0}{X_0}, \tag{4}$$

in which

$$\lambda_t = \frac{\prod_{s=0}^{t} (1 + n_s)}{\prod_{s=0}^{t} (1 + r_s)}; \quad \text{and} \quad z_{96} = \sum_{0}^{1996} \lambda_t \tag{5}$$

(time 0 is December 1982).

6.1.2 Hypotheses on the Debt

The debt D_0 was taken to comprise all maturities (short, medium, and long term) at the end of 1982. We subtracted the value of interest-earning reserves to retain a net debt concept.

One key problem in defining the debt is the concessionality of certain loans. Around 80% of loans to low-income African and Asian countries are extended on concessional terms. Hence their face value does not represent their market value.

To translate their face value to market value, we used the World Bank's "grant element." This indicator gives the relationship between the face value and market value of concessional loans, assuming a nominal market interest rate of 10%. This indicator is calculated as follows: Call P_t the repayments on the concessional loan, L' being the market value.

$$L' = \sum_{t=0}^{\infty} \frac{P_t}{(1 + i)^t},$$

where $i = 10\%$.

The concessionality indicator will be written

$$\mu = 1 - \frac{L'}{L}.$$

(For $\mu = 0$, the market value equals the face value.) Only for the low-income African and Asian countries have we taken the World Bank's grant element.

6.2 The Value of the Index

6.2.1 The Main Results

We now have all the elements needed to calculate b. (The results are given in table 6.1 for each region.) Latin America is the region with the heaviest debt burden. Its solvency index is 13%. All the other regions show values below 10%. For all regions combined, this calculation thus shows that if 13% of their exports go toward repaying their debt, these regions can be declared solvent. We may usefully compare this index to the other measures that are frequently employed. For example, the debt-service ratio for all LDCs was 22.6% in 1981. Our solvency index is less than half that figure for the reasons stated earlier: for a country to be declared solvent, we do not require that it repay the principal or even all of the interest due.

Table 6.1
Value of index b by region

Region	Value of index b
Low-income Asian countries	4.4
Low-income African countries	7.7
Middle-income Asian countries	2.9
Middle-income Sub-Saharan African countries	9.3
Latin America and the Caribbean	13.0
Southern Europe	5.6
North Africa and the Middle East	6.0
Middle-income oil-exporting countries	5.9

Table 6.2
The most unfavorable case by region

Region		Value of index b
Low-income Asian countries	Sudan	22.8
Low-income African countries	Sri Lanka	5.0
Middle-income Asian countries	Philippines	6.8
Middle-income Sub-Saharan African countries	Ivory Coast	15.0
Latin America and the Caribbean	Argentina	16.4
Southern Europe	Turkey	7.7
North Africa and the Middle East	Morocco	11.6
Middle-income oil-exporting countries	Peru	11.1

Among the other regions considered, the middle-income Southeast Asian countries are situated at the bottom end of the spectrum. Their solvency index is under 3%. In view of this, it is not surprising that these countries had no difficulty in raising new loans in 1983 (the Philippines are an exceptional case because political uncertainties brought about a sudden change in attitude on the part of its creditors).

The index for the low-income Asian countries, the middle-income Southern European countries, and the middle-income oil-exporting countries is between 4% and 6%. Africa ranks midway between these regions and Latin America. The low-income African countries have an index of 7.2%, and the middle-income Sub-Saharan African ones have an index of 9.1%.

I give some idea of the variance within each group in table 6.2. The variance is fairly small in Latin America, in low-income Asia, in Southern

Europe, and even in the low-income African countries if we exclude Sudan. On the other hand, table 6.2 also shows that the Philippines, the Ivory Coast, and Peru have a significantly higher debt burden than the regions of Asia, Africa, or the group of oil-exporting countries to which they belong.

I give the value of the solvency index in table 6.3. I break the countries down into three groups, according to whether the index is higher or lower than 6%, or over 13%. Only four countries have a solvency index of over 13%: Sudan (22.8%), Argentina (16.4%), Brazil (15.0%), and the Ivory Coast (15%). With the exception of these four countries, the value of 13% is an upper bound to the cost of debt repayment. The countries that have had to negotiate rescheduling arrangements with their creditors are found for the most part in the second group (index over 6%), with the following handful of exceptions: the Central African Republic, Congo, Gabon, India, Nigeria, Pakistan, Sierra Leone, and Venezuela, which have had to renegotiate their debt despite a solvency index of under 6%. Conversely, the only exceptions among countries with an index of over 6% which have not renegotiated their debt are Mali, Egypt, Israel, and Cameroon. These exceptions are signaled by an asterisk in table 6.3.

We may thus summarize our findings as follows:

PROPOSITION: "Almost always" the cost of debt repayment will absorb less than 15% of the debtor nation's exports; "most" adjustments are in the range of 6 to 15%.

The reader should interpret "almost always" and "most" as he would for a Durbin-Watson test. The thresholds indicated are signals and not necessary or sufficient conditions. If the adjustment (i.e., a current account surplus excluding interest payments) for one country is over 15% of exports, the proposition states that the adjustment will "almost certainly" be satisfactory. If the adjustment is between 6% and 15% of exports, there is good reason to believe that the surplus will be satisfactory. On the other hand, a surplus of less than 6% will probably be too small.

6.3 A Comparison of the Solvency Index with the Adjustment Effort Actually Undertaken in the 1980s

Let us now see, for a selected subgroup of countries, how the adjustment effort actually undertaken by the indebted nations fit the solvency index. In table 6.4, I have calculated the share of each country's exports that has

Table 6.3
Index b of countries' solvency

Group A: $b < 6\%$	Index b
Low-income Asian countries	
Bangladesh	4.60
Burma	5.12
India	3.79
Nepal	0.69
Pakistan	4.02
Low-income African countries	
Central African Republic	3.30
Ethiopia	4.90
Ghana	2.94
Rwanda	0.5
Sierra Leone	5.73
Tanzania	3.75
Middle-income Asian countries	
New Guinea	4.12
Singapore	3.96
Thailand	3.60
Middle-income Sub-Saharan African countries	
Lesotho	0.39
Mauritius	5.67
Seychelles	2.06
Swaziland	1.14
Zimbabwe	5.12
Latin America and the Caribbean	
Bahamas	0.28
Barbados	0.10
Colombia	4.95
El Salvador	3.89
Guatemala	4.70
Paraguay	3.10
Southern Europe	
Cyprus	5.29
Greece	4.57
Malta	3.79
Yugoslavia	3.98
North Africa and Middle East	
Jordan	1.63
Yemen	2.63
Middle-income oil-exporting countries	
Algeria	3.46
Congo*	5.26
Gabon*	1.29
Indonesia	3.24
Malaysia	2.46
Nigeria	3.25
Trinidad	3.16
Tunisia	4.42
Venezuela	5.31

Table 6.3 (continued)

Group B: $6\% < b < 13\%$	
Low-income African countries	
Gambia	9.60
Malawi	7.49
Mali*	6.48
Somalia	9.68
Uganda	8.13
Low-income Asian countries	
Philippines	6.83
Middle-income Sub-Saharan African countries	
Kenya*	6.64
Liberia	11.39
Mauritania	8.12
Zambia	12.94
Latin America and Caribbean	
Bolivia	12.67
Chile	12.01
Costa Rica	12.36
Dominican Republic	7.07
Guyana	8.48
Haiti	9.37
Honduras	9.51
Jamaica	7.26
Uruguay	6.31
Southern Europe	
Israel*	7.12
Portugal*	6.20
Turkey	7.70
North Africa and Middle East	
Morocco	11.63
Middle-income oil-exporting countries	
Cameroon*	6.43
Ecuador	9.73
Egypt*	8.63
Mexico	12.11
Peru	11.17
Group C: $b > 13\%$	
Argentina	16.40
Brazil	15.00
Ivory Coast	14.99
Sudan	22.77

Note: Asterisks denote exceptions: In Group A, the countries whose debt has been rescheduled; in Group B, those whose debt has *not* been rescheduled.

been transferred to creditors over each of the subperiods 1983–1987, 1984–1987, ... 1986–1987. More specifically, for each period $i \in (1983, 1986)$, I have calculated the fraction $\hat{b}_i$ defined as

$$
D_i - \frac{D_{1987}}{\prod\limits_{s=i+1}^{87} (1 + r_s)} = \hat{b}_i \sum_{t=i+1}^{87} \frac{X_t}{\prod\limits_{s=i+1}^{t} (1 + r_s)},
$$

where $\hat{b}_i$ measures the adjustment effort undertaken after time i. Table 6.4 shows that only a subgroup of seven countries out of twenty-four (starred in the table) have adjusted their economies in line with the solvency index over the period 1983–1987. Over the second subperiod 1986–1987, only four out of twenty-four (Chile, Guatemala, Uruguay, and Venezuela) keep passing the test. In particular, Brazil and Mexico passed the test of a successful adjustment over the period under review but failed to maintain the adjustment in the second subperiod. Brazil, for instance, managed to transfer abroad 15% of its exports from 1982 to 1987, which is exactly what the solvency index suggested. Mexico transferred abroad, on average, 18% of its exports over the period 1982–1987, which is above the benchmark suggested by the solvency index.

Over the last years under review, however, Brazil's and Mexico's adjustment efforts fell below the level initially reached (a feature that contradicts Proposition 2 in chapter 5). In the case of Mexico this is no surprise, given the dramatic fall in the price of oil that took place in 1987. Brazil's case is more subtle. On the one hand, it is crucial to note that Brazil's surpluses did *not* go down in 1986 and 1987. The share of Brazil's exports that was transferred abroad was kept at a "healthy" 30%! Despite *negative* net flows of Brazilian debt in 1986 and 1987 (which should have brought *down* the level of debt), Brazil's debt went *up* by 10%. This surprising outcome is in part a reflection of the currency composition of the debt, which increased the dollar value of Brazil's debt as the dollar fell. To the extent that the dollar is a better numeraire of Brazil's exports than other currencies, this can be taken as an unexpected rise in the interest rate faced by Brazil. As such, however, it should be viewed as temporary and should not seriously damage lenders' perception of Brazil's creditworthiness. The next chapter presents an analysis of the domestic counterpart of Brazil's external surplus and uncovers the reasons why lenders did worry about Brazil's creditworthiness and the sustainability of its external surplus.

Table 6.4
b-statistic (%): adjustment in % of exports

%	$\hat{b}_{82}$	$\hat{b}_{83}$	$\hat{b}_{84}$	$\hat{b}_{85}$	$\hat{b}_{86}$	Theoretical b
Algeria	5.46	−2.24	−13.35	−23.68	−19.56	3.4*
Argentina	23.60	22.49	20.80	6.80	−36.87	16.4*
Bolivia	−4.04	10.44	−1.19	2.35	67.32	12.7
Brazil	15.06	13.66	13.06	2.54	−7.82	15.0*
Chile	21.88	21.06	24.96	22.54*	9.18	12.0*
Ivory Coast	−4.78	−15.15	−26.11	−25.91	−42.30	15*
Colombia	−0.96	−1.53	−6.88	−1.61	−5.51	5*
Costa Rica	14.45	21.16	8.99	13.81	10.63	12.4
Ecuador	13.56	4.04	2.61	−6.08	−20.14	9.7
Gabon	−3.89	−9.34	−17.21	−27.26	−24.07	1.3
Guatemala	−4.65	−3.84	5.32	8.78*	12.87	4.7
Honduras	−5.76	−4.76	−10.58	−3.57	−8.27	9.5
Jamaica	1.78	5.54	0.22	3.24	−7.75	7.2
Malawi	2.51	−5.28	−23.41	−26.67	−46.57	7.5
Mexico	18.11	20.64	16.50	11.13	3.88	12.11*
Nicaragua	−12.54	−3.67	−14.95	−37.57	−29.70	3.2
Peru	8.08	−3.29	−8.71	−18.66	−23.45	11.2
Philippines	18.40	13.10	5.47	4.59	12.41	6.8
Senegal	−17.07	−20.19	−32.37	−33.86	−34.33	
Sudan	0.26	−6.42	−5.62	−38.07	−112.66	22.8
Turkey	−12.12	−18.81	−28.49	−34.23	−33.09	7.7
Uruguay*	0.55	8.13	−0.06	11.21	−1.10	6.31
Venezuela	16.23	25.75	23.76	17.35*	7.26	5.31*
Yugoslavia	8.48	7.96	3.06	1.44	−3.89	4*
Zambia	−7.32	−22.42	−51.46	−53.68	−34.62	12.9

6.4 Conclusion

I have sought to demonstrate how an indicator of LDC solvency might be constructed. Using a number of varied assumptions, I have shown that a country's solvency may be analyzed as follows: the country compares the cost of repudiating its external debt to what it would be obliged to forego were it to repay a constant fraction of its resources to its creditors. The country is solvent if the maximum value of this (fixed) fraction compatible with nonrepudiation would effectively enable the debt to be repaid.

On the basis of this analysis I adopted the solvency index as the fraction b of the country's exports that would allow the debt to be repaid. It is this index b that the country must calculate before deciding whether to repudiate or honor its debt. And it is on the basis of an optimum amount b^* that creditors will decide on the maximum amount of credit they are prepared to extend.

This index b, moreover, meets an important criterion: a country would be considered fully creditworthy if its rate of growth was always strictly higher than the international interest rate. This situation, as was seen in chapter 2, cannot occur at equilibrium. It imparts, however, great economic significance (that of the Samuelson model) to the extreme case where it tends toward zero.

From an empirical standpoint, this index allows us to draw the following implications. In general, assigning 15% of exports to debt repayment was a sufficient constraint to ensure the solvency of the developing countries in December 1982. In this respect, a few countries such as Brazil, Mexico, and Venezuela achieved a satisfactory—and even sometimes (in the case of Mexico) an excessive—adjustment in the years that immediately followed the 1982 crisis. As far as these nations are concerned, we may then draw the conclusion that in 1982 those countries were solvent.

7 Domestic and External Debt Constraints

In the previous chapters, it was always assumed that the government was a social planner with an unlimited potential claim on its private citizens' wealth. In this context, the only strategic problem was that arising from the relationship between a government and foreign lenders. In this chapter I take into account the crucial issue of the *domestic* budgetary problem that confronts a government that has to repay its *external* debt.

7.1 Domestic and External Debt: An Accounting Identity

In this chapter I continue to assume that only the government has access to the world financial markets. Under this (strong) hypothesis, a fundamental identity will emerge that will vividly illustrate the link between external and domestic debt problems.

As in the previous chapter, let us consider a one-good exchange economy. Call Q_t the country's total endowment of the good. Let C_t be the private sector's consumption of the good and let G_t represent the government's own consumption. Let us call (as before) D_t the external debt of the government and r_t the world financial market rate of interest at time t. Let us now also take account of the government's domestic debt, B_t, and the domestic real rate of interest, ϱ_t. The main difference between this and the previous approach is that we want to pay explicit attention to the government's domestic budgetary problem. Let us call T_t the amount of taxes collected by the government at time t.

With these definitions and conventions, let us now see how the domestic and the external debt interact. The trade balance and the current account are not different from the previous chapter's definition:

$$TB_t = Q_t - (C_t + G_t).$$

(In an economy without investment, the trade balance is the difference between output and total consumption):

$$CA_t = -(D_t - D_{t-1}) = TB_t - r_t D_{t-1}. \tag{1}$$

The current account (the decrease in the external debt) is the trade balance minus the interest on the debt. A key assumption here is that the foreign debt is borrowed by the government (which can, if it wants, lend it domestically to private investors).

Now the government's overall (foreign and domestic) debt, $D_t + B_t$, follows a law of motion dictated by the government's spending, revenues, and interest due. One can write

$$(D_t + B_t) - (D_{t-1} + B_{t-1}) = G_t - T_t + r_t D_{t-1} + \varrho_t B_{t-1}. \tag{2}$$

On each debt D_t and B_t, the government has imposed the transversality conditions:

$$\lim_{t \to \infty} \frac{D_t}{\prod\limits_{s=1}^{t} (1 + r_s)} = 0; \qquad \lim_{t \to \infty} \frac{B_t}{\prod\limits_{s=1}^{t} (1 + \varrho_s)} = 0. \tag{2'}$$

Substituting $D_t - (D_{t-1} + r_t D_{t-1})$ for what is shown in equation (2), one finds

$$TB_t = (T_t - G_t) + [B_t - (1 + \varrho_t) B_{t-1}]. \tag{3}$$

$T_t - G_t$ is the government's primary surplus (that is, the surplus obtained notwithstanding the interest on the public debt). $B_t - (1 + \varrho_t) B_{t-1}$ measures how much new money the government can drain in net terms from its domestic private sector (taking account of the interest that it must pay). Equation (3) shows that the trade balance is necessarily the counterpart of these two terms.

How does this equality work in the real world? Assume that a country has a trade surplus. If exporters sell their foreign currencies to the central bank, this triggers money creation. If the surplus is monetized, then it appears in equation (3) as part of T_t: it represents a increase in the seigniorage tax of the government. Otherwise, it must be the case that the government has generated a primary surplus and/or that new domestic debt is issued. It is crucial to note that this equality provides no clue as to which causality underlies the trade balance surplus. It can very well be that a large devaluation or direct rationing of imports are the primary forces that have led the economy into a trade surplus. Yet the equality tells us that whatever the cause of a trade surplus, it must necessarily be accompanied by an increase in government domestic debt if it is not accompanied by a government surplus. In short, without a government surplus, total government debt cannot be reduced.

7.2   External Debt with Limited Taxation

7.2.1   A Framework of Analysis

Let us maintain the assumption that only the government has access to the world financial markets so that a discrepancy may arise (we shall see how) between world and domestic interest rates. Were the government to repudiate its external debt, foreign lenders would impose the same penalties as those we assumed before: financial autarky and a direct cost amounting to a fixed fraction of the country's GDP. The riskless rate of interest that prevails worldwide will be assumed to be a constant, r.

To simplify the analysis, assume that the country's GDP is constant, equal to Q, and exogenously endowed to the private sector. The total wealth of the private sector can therefore be measured as

$$W = \sum_{t=0}^{\infty} \frac{1}{\prod_{s=0}^{t} (1 + \varrho_s)} [Q - T_t], \qquad (4)$$

in which T_t is the collection of taxes by the government.

The private sector's interest-bearing financial assets consist of the government's domestic debt B_t. Let us assume that the utility that the private sector derives from consuming C_t is a function $u(C_t)$, which is separable from the provision of public goods whose benefit is directly measured by a function $v(G_t)$. Furthermore (and more arbitrarily), let us assume that the collection of taxes T_t has a welfare-reducing impact that can be directly measured through a loss function $\theta(T_t)$. The private sector's welfare will be assumed to be the algebraic sum of the discounted values of these three terms:

$$J = \sum_{t=0}^{\infty} \beta^t [u(C_t) + v(G_t) - \theta(T_t)].$$

7.2.2   Equilibrium Conditions

As far as the private sector is concerned, distribution of C_t is the only choice that it can make. To the extent that the private sector has access only to the domestic financial market, it will choose an intertemporal pattern (C_t) that is a solution to

$u'(C_t) = \beta(1 + \varrho_t)u'(C_{t+1})$

and subject to its intertemporal budget constraint.

The government must decide to spend G_t, raise T_t, and borrow D_t and B_t abroad and domestically, respectively. It is subject to its own budget constraint (2) and to a credit ceiling $D_t \leqslant \bar{D}_t$, which is imposed by the foreign creditors to keep it from defaulting. Using the identity shown in the previous section, one may simply write the government constraints as follows:

$$
\begin{cases}
(1) \ D_t = (1 + r)D_{t-1} - TB_t \\[2mm]
(2) \ D_t \leqslant \bar{D}_t \\[2mm]
(3) \ B_t = (1 + \varrho_t)B_{t-1} + G_t - T_t + TB_t \\[2mm]
(4) \ \lim_{t \to \infty} \dfrac{1}{\prod\limits_{s=1}^{t}(1 + \varrho_s)} B_t = 0.
\end{cases}
\tag{5}
$$

Whatever the specific (equilibrium) value of $\bar{D}_t$, a key to the government program is as follows: as long as the external debt constraint is not binding, domestic and world interest rates must be equal.

In effect, as long as the constraint on the foreign debt is not binding, the government wants, on the margin, to equate the marginal cost of one more unit of domestic and one more unit of foreign debt. On the other hand, as soon as the external debt becomes rationed, the domestic interest rate jumps: it reflects the need for the country to rely (marginally) on domestic finance only for its intertemporal allocations. If the government is a domestic lender ($D_t \leqslant 0$), this is equivalent to imposing a capital levy on domestic borrowers. If instead the government is a domestic borrower, this is like a *secondary burden* imposed on public finances: the government deficit is suddenly increased because of the jump in the domestic interest rate. In the deterministic economy that we considered, this is a jump that is forecast in advance and that should not be accompanied by a jump in the tax burden. In a stochastic environment, however, an adverse shock may abruptly induce the government to raise the domestic interest rate so as to reflect the sudden rationing of foreign lending.

In the deterministic case that we consider, the government's first-order conditions—as long as the credit ceiling is not binding—can simply be written as

$$\begin{cases} u'(G_t) = \beta(1 + r)u'(G_{t+1}) \\ \theta'(T_t) = \beta(1 + r)\theta'(T_{t+1}). \end{cases} \tag{6}$$

If $\beta(1 + r) < 1$ (a condition we assume), private and public consumption will gradually decline, while domestic taxes will gradually increase. At the time when the credit ceiling binds, the government must generate enough tax resources to service its domestic and foreign debt. In the simple case we examine (with a constant output), the domestic interest rate needs to equal the subjective discount factor so that the following conditions hold:

$$\begin{cases} (1) \ \ C_t = Q - T \\ (2) \ \ T = r\bar{D} + \varrho B \\ (3) \ \ G = Q - C - r\bar{D}. \end{cases} \tag{7}$$

To evaluate which credit ceiling they should impose, lenders must now pay attention, not only to the private sector or the government's spending, but also to the cost of collecting taxes that must accompany the service of the government's foreign and domestic debt. The larger the θ function measuring the welfare-reducing impact of domestic taxation, the lower must be the credit ceiling $\bar{D}$.

7.3 A Comparison of Brazil's and Mexico's Adjustment over the Period 1983–1985

As was emphasized in the previous chapter, both Brazil and Mexico accomplished a very substantial external adjustment during the three years 1983–85. This adjustment was attained by a sharp real devaluation and, notably in the case of Mexico, an abrupt rationing of imports. The question that I want to investigate is the following: Although both countries made the required external adjustment, did governments undertake their own adjustment? Was the secondary burden of raising domestic taxes shouldered?

7.3.1 An Overview

To answer this question, I first decompose government resources into those arising from money creation (the seigniorage tax), which I call $S(t)$, and those arising from the primary surplus, which I call $Z(t)$. (The similarity and difference between seignorage tax and other forms of government taxation are explored in the appendix.) $S(t) + Z(t)$ is therefore the overall

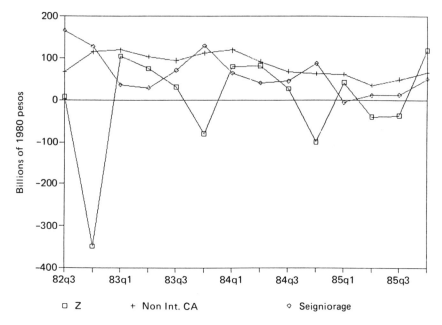

Figure 7.1
Mexico—quarterly data, 1982–1985

government surplus, $T(t) - G(t)$ in equation (3). This last equation can therefore be written

$$TB(t) = S(t) + Z(t) + [B(t) - (1 + \varrho_t)B(t - 1)]. \tag{8}$$

As was already emphasized, equation (8) states that a trade surplus is necessarily accompained by: 1. money creation, 2. a government primary surplus, 3. an increase of domestic debt, or a combination of these three items. Each of these items is plotted in figures 7.1 and 7.2, which illustrate the cases of Brazil and Mexico, respectively.

In the case of Brazil, we can distinguish two stages in the adjustment pattern. In 1983, the noninterest payment current account surplus was accompanied by a sharp rise of the government primary surplus. (This period corresponds to the time of the IMF program.) But the peak is attained in the last quarter of 1983, and from then on, government primary surplus has been declining almost steadily. By contrast, the seigniorage tax has followed very closely the variations in the current account, leaving

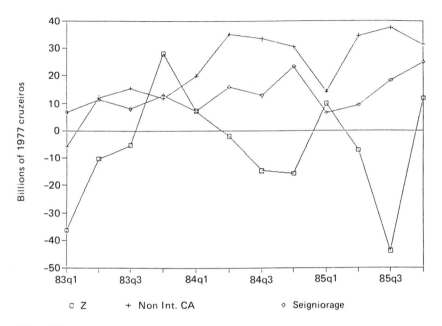

Figure 7.2
Brazil—quarterly data, 1983–1985

little doubt that the external surplus has been monetized through the purchase by the central bank of the dollars earned by exporters. Mexico's adjustment is less extreme than Brazil's. The government primary surplus exhibits a cyclical pattern, being in surplus in the first three quarters of each year and in deficit in the fourth (an exception is 1985). Furthermore, even though the seigniorage tax amounts to a very substantial part of the external surplus, it is not as closely related to the variations of the latter as in Brazil.

The comparison between the government effort in both countries is best summarized by figures 7.3 and 7.4. Mexico has been able to curb total government debt, while Brazil's overall government debt has kept rising over all three years under review.

7.3.2 A Decomposition

To assess quantitatively the decomposition of the adjustment, I add up equation (8) as follows:

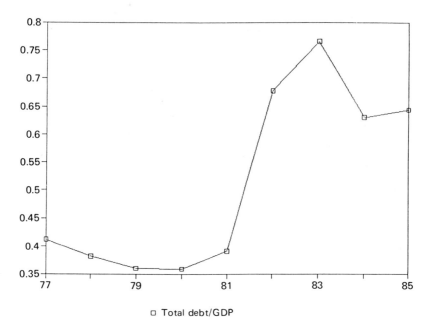

Figure 7.3
Mexico—total debt/GDP, 1977–1985

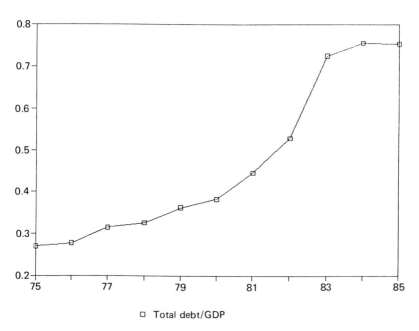

Figure 7.4
Brazil—total debt/GDP, 1975–1985

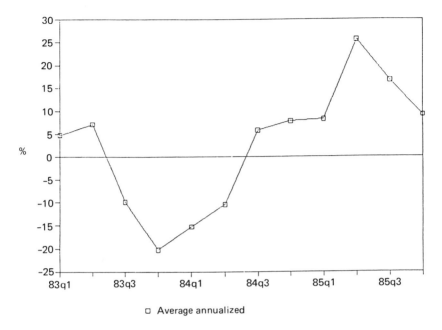

Figure 7.5
Brazil—quarterly average ex-post real rate, 1983–1985

$$\sum_{t=1}^{T} \frac{TB(t)}{\prod_{i=1}^{t}(1+\varrho_i)} = \sum_{t=1}^{T} \frac{S(t)}{\prod_{i=1}^{t}(1+\varrho_i)} + \sum_{t=1}^{T} \frac{Z(t)}{\prod_{i=1}^{t}(1+\varrho_i)} + B(0) - \frac{B(T)}{\prod_{i=1}^{T}(1+\varrho_i)},$$

in which $t = 1$ corresponds to the first quarter of 1983 and $t = T$ correspond to the fourth quarter of 1985. The left-hand side is the discounted sum of the external surpluses; the right-hand side is the sum of government revenues generated by seigniorage, the primary surplus, and the net increase of government domestic debt. Taking the left-hand side as the scale factor, the decomposition evolves numerically as follows: In the case of Brazil, the seigniorage tax amounts to 57.5% of the external adjustment, the domestic debt increase amounts to 71.0%, and the primary surplus of the government amounts to *minus* 28.6%. Taking $Z + S$ as the measure of government total income, 29% of the external surplus was really paid for by the government and 71% was financed by domestic debt. In other words, the secondary burden of raising taxes in order to service the government's external debt has not been borne in the case of Brazil.

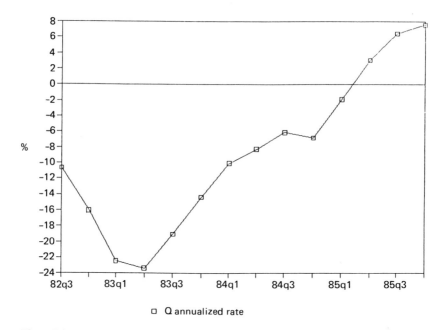

Figure 7.6
Mexico—quarterly average real rate, 1982–1985

The same decomposition in the case of Mexico yields the following results: The seigniorage tax amounts to 93% of the external balance surplus. The primary surplus amounts to −8.6%, while the domestic debt increase amounts to 15.2%. Taking the seigniorage tax and the primary surplus as the measure of government income, one sees that 85% of the trade surplus has been financed through taxation.

It is not surprising, under these circumstances, to find a very different pattern for the real domestic interest in each country (see figures 7.5 and 7.6). Expect for 1985, real rates have been very substantially negative in Mexico while, except for 1983, they have been very substantially positive in Brazil. Brazil rapidly entered into a vicious cycle. Real rates were around 20% and domestic debt represented 33% of GDP. Real interest payments on the domestic debt alone therefore represented 6.6% of GDP.

7.3.3 The Seigniorage Tax

Brazil's difficulties were further complicated by the increased inefficiency of the seigniorage tax. As is well known, there is a maximum bound to the

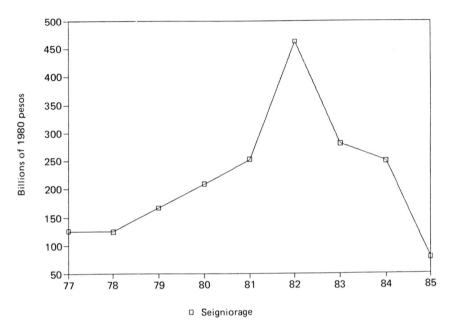

Figure 7.7
Mexico—seigniorage, 1977–1985

real income that a government can extract from money creation. The corresponding maximum rate of inflation is equal to the inverse of the semi-elasticity of money demand with respect to nominal interest rates. In the case of Brazil, rough estimates indicate that the inflation rate came very near that point. (The estimated value of the monthly semi-elasticity is 0.77, which implies a maximum monthly inflation rate of 11%—very near the actual rate reached in 1985.) Direct evidence confirms this point. While the inflation rate doubled after the 1982 crisis, seigniorage revenues were raised by only 17% in Brazil.

In Mexico, the government seems to have enjoyed a much larger degree of freedom in this respect. As we have indicated, seigniorage amounted to a very substantial part of the trade surplus. Yet, as figures 7.7–7.10 show, both inflation and the seigniorage tax itself were rapidly decreasing during the period under review. Most of the gains have been concentrated in 1982 and in the beginning of 1983. It seems to be the case that the sharp 1982 inflation took the private sector by surprise and helped the government to

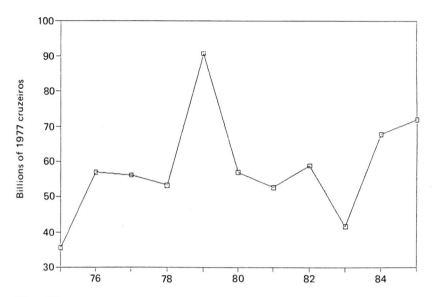

Figure 7.8
Brazil—seigniorage, 1976–1984

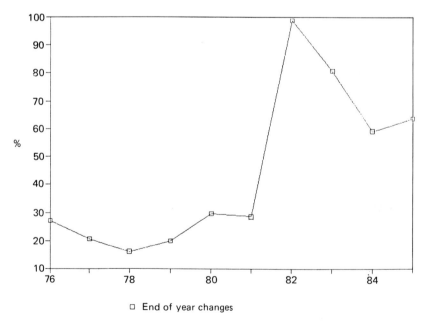

□ End of year changes

Figure 7.9
Mexico—annual inflation, 1976–1984

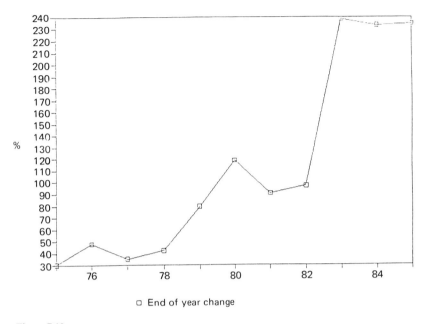

Figure 7.10
Brazil—annual inflation, 1976–1984

finance easily the bulk of the 1982–83 adjustment. This is a luxury that the indexed Brazilian economy has not been able to afford.

In both cases, this decomposition reveals the importance of the seigniorage tax in total government revenue. In both instances, any attempt to force the government to reach a monetary target would have been disastrous. In the balance of evils, inflation must be carefully weighed against rising domestic debt and rising real interest rates. Here, any use of the monetary approach to the balance of payment might be very harmful if it were to imply that monetary restraint is the appropriate tool for managing the external debt.

7.4   Conclusion

Brazil's crisis has been shown to stem from the government's insolvency, *not* from the insolvency of the nation. In 1985, Brazil reached the point where repaying more external debt became potentially extremely damaging to its domestic economy and became counterproductive. As I have shown, it is a process that augmented (almost one-to-one) the government domestic debt by the same amount as the service of the external debt. In chapter 6 I argued that committing 15% of Brazil's export revenues to debt servicing was sufficient to guarantee the country's external solvency. If this policy had been adopted, domestic debt would have risen much more moderately, by 22% instead of the actual 80% that was experienced from 1982 to 1985.

If one trusts this analysis, one can make the point that in the case of Brazil, *less* foreign debt and *more* domestic debt needed to be serviced in the period 1982–85. If one takes the view adopted in this chapter—according to which tax collection is intrinsically welfare reducing—a program delivering *more* taxes must indeed be accompanied by *more* private consumption and a correspondingly lower trade balance. The intuition suggested by the calculations presented in this chapter is that such a program would have been Pareto-improving.

As far as Mexico is concerned, it was *not* found that domestic considerations played the same counterproductive role as in the case of Brazil. The origin of Mexico's debt servicing problems must be sought elsewhere. It does not take long to find the likely candidate: the extreme volatility of Mexico's terms of trade. The price of oil fell by more than half from 1985 to 1987, making the initial adjustment—however satisfactory it may have been, both externally and domestically—incapable of resisting such violent fluctuations. If one takes the downfall of the price of oil as permanent, or quasi-permanent, the following question arises: Shouldn't Mexico's debt now be scaled down on Mexico's resources? Even though the price of oil may go up, will it not be the case that the burden of the debt will create a profound disincentive to adjust and prove counterproductive to the lenders themselves? These are some of the questions that will be reviewed in the final part of this book.

Appendix: Money Creation as a Substitute for Government's Direct Taxation

When a country reaches a trade surplus, the first instinct of a debt-laden government is to exchange the hard currency earned by exporters for domestic money. If this is not sterilized, it is nothing but a pure taxation device. Who actually pays the tax, and which distortions does it involve? These are the question that this appendix will briefly address.

Money as a Tax: The Consumer's View

When a private agent holds money (for whatever purpose), it loses the interest that any alternative store of value would yield. More specifically, holding money rather than an interest-bearing asset amounts to: 1. losing the real interest rate paid on an alternative asset; 2. foregoing the purchasing power of money that is lost to inflation (if there is any). The sum of these two compounds is the nominal interest rate, which measures the opportunity cost of holding money.

The explanation of why agents hold money rather than an interest-bearing asset, is that money performs a role that no other interest-bearing asset does. Rather than entering into the debate of what this function is, I will simply assume arbitrarily (à la Clower) that some of the transactions that are made by private agents must be paid in *cash*, which is why private agents must keep some of it in their pockets. I will also make the restrictive assumption that the government has the *monopoly* on issuing the cash needed by the private sector.

Call $h(C_t)$ the amount of cash that private agents need to pay up front in order to consume C_t. I will write this cash-in-advance constraint as

$$h(C_t) \leqslant \frac{M_t}{P_t}, \tag{1}$$

in which M_t is the nominal stock of money kept by the private sector during time t in order to consume C_t. P_t is the price level that prevails at that time. $1/P(t)$ is the purchasing power, at time t, of one unit of cash. Call W_t the interest-bearing asset held by the agent; $W_t + [M(t)/P(t)]$ is how much wealth the agents holds by the end of time t. The law of motion of this total wealth can be written

$$W(t) + \frac{M(t)}{P(t)} = [1 + r_t]W(t-1) + \frac{M(t-1)}{P(t)} - C_t. \tag{2}$$

To remain solvent, an agent's intertemporal decisions must obey the transversality condition

$$\lim_{t \to \infty} \frac{W_t}{\prod_{s=1}^{t}(1 + r_s)} = 0,$$

and he must satisfy the cash-in-advance constraint written in (3). Let us assume that the private agent wants to

$$\text{Maximize} \sum_{1}^{\infty} \beta^t u(C_t),$$

subject to both the solvency and the liquidity constraint. The first-order conditions associated with this program can be written[1]

$$u'(C_t) = \lambda_t [1 + h'(C_t) \cdot i_t], \tag{3}$$

in which λ_t in the shadow price associated with the solvency constraint of the agent. The marginal utility of consumption is the sum of two terms: 1. the marginal utility of wealth, λ_t, and 2. the marginal cost of holding money associated with one more unit of consumption, $\lambda_t \cdot h'(C_t) \cdot i_t$.

The nominal interest rate can be seen as a wedge between the price of consumption and its shadow price to the consumer. It is distortionary if and only if $i_t h'(C_t) \neq 0$.

From the viewpoint of the consumer, money is a sort of value-added tax (taken on the part of his consumption that must be paid in cash) whose shadow cost is $i_t [M(t)]/[P(t)]$.

Seigniorage and the Government's Income

The consumer acts as if the price of "cash goods" was inflated by the nominal rate of interest; what is the benefit that the government obtains from the creation of money?

At each time t, the government issues $H(t) = M(t) - M(t - 1)$ and, in purchasing power terms, it receives $[H(t)]/[P(t)]$. When all incomes accruing to the government are taken into account, they generate the following revenue:

$$W_m = \frac{M(0)}{P(0)} + \sum_{t=1}^{\infty} \frac{M(t+1) - M(t)}{P(t+1)} \frac{1}{\prod_{s=1}^{t}(1 + r_s)}. \tag{4}$$

Rearranging terms, one finds

$$W_m = \sum_{t=1}^{\infty} i_t \frac{M(t)}{P(t)} \frac{1}{\prod_{s=1}^{t}(1 + r_s)}. \tag{5}$$

The government therefore exactly collects, over time, the cost foregone by the consumer in order to pay some of its consumption in cash.

This identity between government revenues generated by money creation and the opportunity cost foregone by consumers is fundamental. It shows that money creation is not essentially different from any other tax system: the distortion it induces on the relative price structure is exactly the counterpart to the revenues collected by the government.

Yet this identity hides an important difference between the time pattern of the cost borne by consumers and the revenues gained by the government. On a *flow* basis, the distortion induced by nominal interest rate appears at each time t. On the other hand, on a period-by-period basis, the government does not earn $i_t(M_t/P_t)$ but $[M(t + 1) - M(t)]/[P(t)]$, which need not coincide. Consider for instance a stationary state economy in which the government sets a constant growth rate of the money supply π (equal to the equilibrium inflation rate) while the private sector holds a stationary stock of cash balance $m = M/P$. In such a case, the government collects $\pi \cdot m$ each period while consumers forego $i \cdot m$. The difference between the two, $r \cdot m$, is the real interest rate foregone by holding m every period. Where has this difference gone? The answer is apparent from equation (4). The seignorage tax collected by the government has two components: the stock of money issued in the past (m) and the flow increases that occur to the government every period. The past collection of seigniorage m is equivalent to a flow of resources $r \cdot m$ every period. While this is a cost that each private consumer takes into account on a period-by-period basis, it does not constitute a source of *new* government benefit.

IV LARGE DEBT AND SLOW GROWTH

The 1980s witnessed a spectacular decrease in the growth rate of the LDCs, which has fallen from an average of 7% in the period 1974–80 to 3.4% in the 1980s. For the highly indebted countries (HICs), the decline is more spectacular: the growth rate fell from 6% to 1.1% for the corresponding periods. This casual comparison suggests that the HICs have been hit more dramatically than the other LDCs. Direct evidence on Latin American countries, in particular, also seems to suggest that the attempt to service the debt created tremendous domestic pressures that eventually brought down investment and the growth rate. In the LDC debt literature, this negative correlation between debt and growth has been known as a "debt overhang" problem (see Sachs 1988). Debt is akin to a tax on the domestic economy and too much of it may sometimes create a "debt Laffer curve" problem (see Krugman 1988).

Most empirical analysis relying on this interpretation hinges on a comparison between growth and investment rates that prevailed before and after the 1982 debt crisis. Such comparisons are not well taken, however, to the extent that they overlook the formidable change of regime that took place for all countries (however indebted they may have been) before and after that period. As was emphasized in chapter 2, the years from the onset of the oil crisis to the early 1980s may indeed be characterized as a period of relatively free access to the world financial markets in which an extremely low—indeed perhaps negative—real interest rate prevailed. The years following 1982 could be roughly characterized instead as a period during which the abrupt rise of the world interest rate shut off most countries' access to the financial markets, a switch that is unambiguously adverse to growth, however indebted the country may have been at the time of the switch (see the discussion in chapter 9).

It is a second effect of the switch of regime from the 1970s into the 1980s that is referred to in the debt overhang literature: the highly indebted countries had to precipitously repay their debt, in addition to being kept from borrowing new resources. The impact of this second effect on growth and investment, however, is ambiguous and depends on the efficiency of the rescheduling process. At any rate, it must be carefully distinguished from the first effect, which can roughly be characterized as a return to a kind of financial autarky. In light of this distinction, I will discuss how beneficial to the debtors (and perhaps to the banks themselves) a partial write-off of the debt may be.

8 Growth and External Debt

Large debts reduce growth. This is a statement that the 1980s seem to make uncontroversial. Yet in a Fisherian ("perfect capital market") view of the world, it is a proposition that does not hold. If growth is taken to be driven by capital accumulation, the separation of the firms' decision to invest from any debt-related issues (the firms' own debt or the rest of the nation's debt) makes the growth rate of an economy independent of its external debt (and only a function of the discrepancy between the domestic productivity of capital and the world interest rate). In contrast, when the risk of debt repudiation is taken into consideration, the credit rationing that this threat imposes on the country straightforwardly explains the negative correlation between growth and debt.

In this chapter, I present a model (from Cohen and Sachs 1986) in which capital accumulation is the only force driving growth. It shares many of the insights spelled out in Romer 1986 and 1987, in that stable endogenous growth will be obtained as the outcome of a constant-return-to-scale technology of production in the storable asset. I shall characterize three regimes to which a small country may adhere: one of financial autarky, in which domestic saving must match the accumulation of capital; one of free access to the world financial markets, in which foreign saving can finance without bound any profitable domestic investment; and finally, one with limited access to world financial markets, in which the restriction is (endogenously) determined by the threat of debt repudiation. In this chapter, I analyze only the credit constraint that lenders can *efficiently* impose on the country, postponing until chapter 9 the discussion of alternative equilibria in which an inefficient debt overhang may occur.

The key result shown in that chapter is that constrained access to the world financial markets sets the growth rate of the domestic economy in between the rate that prevails in the two extreme cases when access to the markets is entirely free and when there is financial autarky. In the early stage of the borrowing process, the growth rate is perhaps near but certainly always below the first rate; in the late stage it is always *above* the second one: repaying one's debt should not crowd *out* investment, rather it should crowd it *in*. The intuition behind this perhaps surprising result is as follows: lenders are less impatient than the debtor; they value growth of the indebted economy more than the debtor itself. When they are able to reschedule the debt efficiently, they want to induce the country to invest *more* than it would at financial autarky. We shall see in chapter 9 how an inefficient rescheduling may yield—in the last stage of the borrowing process—an equilibrium growth rate that is *below* the autarkic level.

8.1 The Setup

(a) **Production**   I will consider a one-good economy, in which the same good can be indifferently used for export, consumption, or investment. Each period, the available stock of capital is a predetermined variable. The production Q_t is a linear function of existing capital:

$$Q_t = aK_t. \tag{1}$$

Capital can be increased through investment, and investment itself is a costly process. Let us assume (following Abel 1978 and Hayashi 1982) that an increase I_t of capital costs J_t:

$$J_t = I_t\left(1 + \frac{1}{2}\phi\frac{I_t}{K_t}\right). \tag{2}$$

The investment decision I_t, while taken at time t, increases the capital stock at time $t + 1$, according to the law of motion:

$$K_{t+1} = K_t(1 - d) + I_t, \tag{3}$$

in which d is the rate of depreciation of installed capital. As one sees from equations (1) to (3), the technology of production exhibits a constant-return-to-scale feature. (Doubling the capital stock and the investment rate would double output and keep the growth rate unchanged.) For that reason, our model will be akin to that suggested in Romer 1986 and 1987 to explain endogenous growth. In Romer's models (as well as that in Barro 1989), the reason the growth rate is not infinite is due to the limited amount of savings, which raises interest rates to the point where the growth rate is stabilized. Such a model would be ill-suited to analyze the free access of a small country to world financial markets (on which the interest rates is taken as a constant that does not depend upon the country's debt). In our model, the growth rate is intrinsically bounded by the adjustment cost

$$\left(\frac{1}{2}\phi\frac{I_t^2}{K_t}\right),$$

which limits—for a given stock of installed capital—the opportunity to invest too fast.

(b) **Preferences**   I will assume that the country is managed by a social planner who can impose investment and consumption decisions on the country. The planner's preferences are represented by an intertemporal utility function:

$$U_0 = \sum_0^\infty \beta^t u(C_t),\tag{5}$$

in which C_t is the aggregate consumption of the country at time t; and $u(C) = (1/\gamma)C^\gamma$, $\gamma < 1$ and $\gamma \neq 0$, or $u(C) = \mathrm{Log}\, C$ when $\gamma = 0$.

One could assume as well that domestic financial markets are efficient *and* that the government can decentralize any aggregate credit constraint along the lines spelled out in chapter 3.

(c) External Debt Just as in the previous chapters, I assume that the country has access to the world financial markets, on which a riskless rate of interest r prevails, and may repudiate its external debt. The two sanctions following the repudiation of the debt will be as in the previous chapters:

(i) A defaulting country is forced to financial autarky forever after it has defaulted.
(ii) The productivity of capital of the defaulting country is reduced by a factor λ so that the post-default technology of production is:

$$Q_t = (1 - \lambda)aK_t.\tag{6}$$

In all that follows, I will assume that the lenders are risk-neutral, act competitively, and have access to the riskless rate of interest, r, which stays constant. I will assume that β is below $1/(1 + r)$ to ensure that the country will be constrained on the borrowing side. Furthermore, I will leave aside all bargaining issues and assume that the lenders can credibly make (at each point in time, but not necessarily for the entire future) a take-it-or-leave-it offer to the debtor (other technical conditions needed to reach an equilibrium are stated in appendix A).

8.2 Two Extreme Cases: Financial Autarky and Free Access to the World Financial Markets

In this section, I would like to calculate the optimal investment strategy in the two extreme cases: when the country is forced to financial autarky, and when it has free access to the world financial markets.

8.2.1 Financial Autarky

Assume first that the country has *no* access to the world financial markets. Domestic investment must be financed out of domestic saving and the

planner (or for that matter, the domestic financial market) solve the following program:

$$U(Q_0) \equiv \underset{(J_t)_{t \geq 0}}{\text{Max}} \sum_0^\infty \beta^t u[Q_t - J_t], \tag{7}$$

subject to (1)–(3).

The solution is shown (in appendix A) to involve a *fixed* investment rate,
x_0:

$$\frac{I_t}{Q_t} = x_0, \qquad \forall t, \tag{8}$$

so that the equilibrium growth rate of the economy is also a constant:

$$n_0 = ax_0 - d. \tag{9}$$

When this equilibrium rate is chosen, equation (7) can be shown to deliver
the following utility level:

$$U_0(Q_0) = C_0 Q_0^\gamma \quad \text{if } \gamma \neq 0 \qquad \text{or}$$

$$U_0(Q_0) = \frac{1}{1 - \beta} \text{Log } Q_0 + C_0 \quad \text{if } \gamma = 0, \tag{10}$$

in which C_0 is a constant that depends upon (a, ϕ, β, γ).

Out of this analysis, it is also straightforward to find the equilibrium that
would prevail after a country has defaulted on its external debt. Indeed,
the equilibrium is simply that which a country whose technology of production is

$$Q_t = a(1 - \lambda)K_t$$

would reach when at financial autarky. We can therefore characterize the
post-default utility level as

$$\left\{ \begin{array}{ll} U_d(Q_0) = C_d Q_0^\gamma & \text{if } \gamma \neq 0 \\[2mm] U_d(Q_0) = \dfrac{1}{1 - \beta} \text{Log } Q_0 + C_d & \text{if } \gamma = 0, \end{array} \right. \tag{11}$$

in which C_d is a function that obivously satisfies $C_d < C_0$.

8.2.2   The Open Economy Case

Assume in this subsection that $\lambda = 1$ in equation (6) above, that is, assume that the country cannot repudiate its external debt (because it is too costly). With that assumption, the model boils down to the standard Fisherian case where the investment decision can be separated from the consumption decision. I will simply solve, here, the optimal investment decision. The country wants to maximize its productive wealth when the return on its investment is taken to be the world riskless rate of interest. Mathematically, this amounts to solving the following program:

$$W_0 = \underset{(I_t)_{t \geq 0}}{\mathrm{Max}} \left\{ \sum_0^\infty \frac{1}{(1 + r)^t} \left[aK_t - I_t \left(1 + \frac{1}{2} \phi \frac{I_t}{K_t} \right) \right] \right\}. \tag{12}$$

The solution to this program is given in appendix A. Given the linearities in the model, W_0 is shown to be a linear function of initial output:

$$W_0 = \bar{\omega} Q_0. \tag{13}$$

It is obtained by picking up a fixed investment rate

$$\bar{x} = \frac{I_t}{Q_t} \tag{14}$$

associated with a fixed rate of gross investment:

$$\bar{y} = \frac{J_t}{Q_t} = \bar{x}(1 + \tfrac{1}{2}\phi a \bar{x}) \tag{15}$$

(The technical conditions necessary for the existence of the equilibrium are spelled out in appendix A.) I refer to this equilibrium as *the socially efficient equilibrium*. It is the equilibrium that would be attained in a free-trade world without nations.

In the case when $\beta < 1/(1 + r)$ and when $\bar{x} \geq d$, which we shall assume, the equilibrium growth rate is larger with free access to financial markets than under financial autarky.

8.3   Efficient Credit Ceilings

Let us now consider the case in which the country has limited access to the world financial markets. Because of the threat of debt repudiation (assuming $\lambda < 1$), lenders cannot afford to let the country invest at the socially efficient rate. Indeed, if they were to do so, the country would necessarily prefer to default rather than service its debt (this is shown in section 8.4.2). To find how lenders should operate to keep the country from defaulting, we shall proceed as follows. First, we shall assume that the lenders can monitor the country's economy (except for its decision to default) and calculate which investment rate they would want the country to choose in order to maximize the present value of the transfers paid by the debtor. Second, we shall see how they should set the credit ceiling to attain this (constrained) preferred equilibrium.

8.3.1 Maximizing the Country's Repayments

In this section, I will consider the following simple problem. Assume that the face value of the debt is infinite and assume that the lenders can monitor both the investment and the repayment strategy of the debtor in such a way as to maximize the value of the transfers made abroad by the country. While the borrower will be assumed to give up sovereignty over its consumption and investment decisions, it will nevertheless preserve sovereignty over the matter of defaulting: at any point in time, the borrower will be free to break the lenders' rule and to follow the post-default path defined by equation (12). In other words, the rules of the game in this section are as follows: the lenders monitor the debtor's economy to maximize the value of the transfers channelled abroad by the debtor, subject to the constraint that the program is never expected (either today or later on) to be dominated by a post-default path. Clearly, under this set of hypothesis, the value of the transfers channelled abroad by the debtor will provide an upper bound to the market value of any debt accumulated by the country.

Formally, the problem can be written as follows. Call P_t the transfers abroad made by the debtor, y_t the gross investment rate (inclusive of the cost of installation) achieved by the country, and C_t the consumption left to the country. One has

$$C_t = Q_t(1 - y_t) - P_t.$$

Call

$$U_t = \sum_{s=t}^{\infty} \beta^{s-t} u(C_s) \tag{16}$$

the level of utility that the lenders' program is expected to deliver to the country. With these notations, the program the lenders must solve is to

$$\text{Maximize } \sum_{t=0}^{\infty} \frac{P_t}{(1+r)^t}, \tag{17}$$

subject to $U_t \geq U_d(Q_t)$, for all t, in which $U_d(Q_t)$ is the post-default level of utility, as defined in equation (11).

This problem is solved in appendix B. Given the many linearities built into this model, the problem boils down to finding a fixed (gross) investment rate y and a fixed debt service ratio P_t/Q_t that solves problem (17). The solution is shown to involve an investment rate that lies between the socially efficient rate and the financial autarky rate. One can state:

PROPOSITION 1:   The "maximum repayment" program the lenders would like to monitor involves a fixed investment rate that is smaller than the socially optimum one and larger than the financial autarky equilibrium rate. It involves a transfer of resources that is a fixed fraction of GDP, a fraction that is smaller than the cost of default.

From Proposition 1, one therefore sees that the banks, even when they can design the investment and consumption policy of the borrower, choose a lower investment rate than that which is socially desirable. The reason is that the banks must take care to avoid the possibility that the country may one day choose to default. A too-rapid path of capital accumulation, even while socially desirable, will raise the post-default utility of the country and, if not carefully balanced, can be counterproductive to the banks.

8.3.2   How Should the Credit Ceiling Be Set?

Let us now see how the debt should be constrained and refinanced to make sure that: 1. the country never chooses to default, and 2. the debt ceiling is at the maximum value above which the country would default and below which the repayments made by the debtor would fall short of the maximum calculated in the previous section.

Whatever its precise value, call $U(D_{t-1}, Q_t)$ the best utility the country could reach when it has accumulated a debt D_{t-1}, and can produce Q_t. Keeping the country from defaulting amounts to find a lending strategy such that

$U(D_{t-1}, Q_t) \geqslant U_d(Q_t) \quad \forall t,$

in which $U_d(Q_t)$ is the post-default reservation level [calculated in equation (11)]. Because of the linearity of the model, this is an inequality that can be conjectured to take the form

$$D_{t-1} \leqslant h^* Q_t \qquad (18)$$

for some (unknown) equilibrium value of h^*. As shown in appendix B, such an inequality gives in fact the answer to the *two* questions raised at the beginning of this section: 1. To avoid default, the lenders should impose a credit ceiling that takes the form of an upper bound to the debt-to-GDP ratio; 2. they should reschedule the debt to keep this ratio a constant in order to induce the country to choose the investment strategy that they would like to design themselves. When h^* is the maximum value compatible with nonrepudiation, the constrained first best is attained. Taking for granted that the debt-to-GDP ratio will be kept constant, the country knows that it will have to pay the creditors (when n is the growth rate of the economy)

$$P_t = [r - n]D_{t-1} = (r - n)h^* Q_t, \qquad (19)$$

so that the country now consumes

$$C_t = Q_t[1 - y_t - (r - n)h^*]. \qquad (20)$$

The social planner selects a rate of growth n^* that is the best possible, that is, one that solves

$$U_{h^*}(Q) = \text{Maximize} \sum_{t=0}^{\infty} \beta^t u[C_t] \text{ subject to } D_{t-1} = h^* Q_t. \qquad (21)$$

In turn, the equilibrium value h^* that the lenders will impose is one such that

$$U_{h^*}(Q) = U_d(Q).$$

For that value of h^*, the equilibrium attained by the country is nothing but the maximum repayment strategy that was calculated in the previous subsection. Where does the equilibrium investment rate lie when the credit ceiling binds? One can show (see appendix C) that the constrained investment rate is in fact an *increasing* function of the credit ceiling h^*. From this perspective, debt crowds *in* investment. In particular, the constrained investment rate is *above* the financial autarky rate (which corresponds to the case when $h^* = 0$). We can state the following proposition.

PROPOSITION 2:   When the debt is efficiently rescheduled, the service of the debt crowds *in* domestic investment.

8.4   The Transition from Small to Large Debt

8.4.1   First-Order Optimality Conditions

Now that we have characterized how the optimal credit ceiling should be set, we can spell out the dynamics of debt and growth from the time a country enters the world financial markets to the point at which it reaches its credit ceiling. Formally, the optimal transition path is obtained by solving the following program:

$$\text{Maximize } \sum_0^\infty \beta^t u(C_t)$$

subject to

$$
\begin{cases}
\text{(a)} \ K_{t+1} = K_t(1 - d) + I_t \\[2mm]
\text{(b)} \ D_t = (1 + r)D_{t-1} + C_t + I_t\left(1 + \frac{1}{2}\phi \frac{I_t}{K_t}\right) - aK_t \\[2mm]
\text{(c)} \ D_{t-1} \leqslant h^* a K_t.
\end{cases}
\qquad (22)
$$

Call μ_t, λ_t, and v_t the Lagrange multiplier associated with each of the three constraints.

The first-order condition can be written

$$
\begin{cases}
\text{(a)} \ \lambda_t = u'(C_t) \\[2mm]
\text{(b)} \ I_t = \frac{1}{\phi}\left(\frac{\mu_t}{\lambda_t} - 1\right) \\[2mm]
\text{(c)} \ \mu_{t-1} = \beta\left[(1 - d)\mu_t + \lambda_t \frac{1}{2}\phi\left(\frac{I_t}{K_t}\right)^2 + a\lambda_t + v_t h^* a\right] \\[2mm]
\text{(d)} \ \lambda_t = \beta(1 + r)\lambda_{t+1} + v_t \\[2mm]
\text{(e)} \ v_t(D_{t-1} - h^* a K_t) = 0.
\end{cases}
\qquad (23)
$$

As long as the credit ceiling $D_{t-1} \leqslant h^*aK_t$ is not reached, the multiplier v_t is nil. To describe the transition from the time the debt is nil to the point at which it has reached its credit ceiling, we can set $v_t = 0$ in the equation above.

8.4.2 Consumption

From equations (23a) and (23b), one finds that the law of motion of consumption obeys the usual first-order condition:

$$u'(C_t) = \beta(1 + r)u'(C_{t+1}).$$ (24)

To the extent that we have restricted our analysis to the case in which $\beta < 1/(1 + r)$ (the country is a "debtor"), consumption is decreasing over time (as long as the credit ceiling is not binding).

This equation shows why the credit ceiling will necessarily be binding at one point in time whenever the cost of debt repudiation is strictly smaller than 1. Indeed, if not, the law of motion (24) would depict the full dynamics of consumption over time. Consumption would therefore converge toward zero in the long run, as debt is accumulated. It would then necessarily be the case that the country would be better off by defaulting and consuming a strictly positive fraction of its stock of capital.

When the credit ceiling is binding, consumption—as well as investment and debt—grows at the same speed as the economy (along the maximum repayment scheme depicted in the previous section). (The value of the multiplier v_t imposes such a law of motion.)

8.4.3 Investment

Call $q_t = \mu_t/\lambda_t$ the shadow price of capital when the marginal utility of consumption is taken as the numeraire. From equation (23c), one sees that investment is simply a linear function of q:

$$\frac{I_t}{K_t} = \frac{1}{\phi}(q_t - 1).$$ (25)

(This result follows Abel 1978 and Hayashi 1982 and gives a specific content to Tobin's q theory.) q_t follows a law of motion that is depicted through equations (23b) and (23d):

$$q_t = \frac{1}{1 + r}\left[(1 - d)q_{t+1} + a + \frac{1}{2}\phi x_{t+1}^2\right]$$ (26)

It is a forward-looking variable that depends on productivity and on a term $\frac{1}{2}\phi x_t^2$, which measures the positive effect of investing today on the future costs of capital installation. The system is closed by imposing that the value q_T at the time the credit ceiling binds corresponds to the investment rate obtained in the maximum repayment scheme.

q_T is therefore simply calculated as a solution to

$$x^* = \frac{1}{\phi}(q_T - 1), \tag{27}$$

in which x^* is the investment rate picked up by the country when the credit ceiling binds. From this terminal value of q_T, one can therefore obtain

$$q_t = \sum_{s=t+1}^{T} \frac{1}{(1 + r)^s} \left[a + \frac{1}{2}\phi x_{s+1}^2 \right] + \frac{1}{(1 + r)^T} q_T. \tag{28}$$

The further away T, the larger the value of q_t.

From these dynamics, one also sees that the larger the debt-output ratio, the sooner the credit ceiling is expected to bind and the lower the value of q. The larger the debt, the lower the investment rate, hence the lower the growth rate of the economy. The equation "large debt implies slow growth" has been proved (for a *given* country).

Furthermore, equation (28) can help make the two following statements. The value of q_0 is always below the value that would be attained when the country has free access to the world financial markets (which would correspond to $T = +\infty$). Hence, investment is always below the socially efficient level. In the early stage of the borrowing process, however, simulation studies (presented in Cohen and Sachs 1986) show that for reasonable values of the parameters, investment is near that level.

Second, investment eventually reaches, at time T, the maximum repayment solution. It is therefore above the financial autarky level, as shown in Proposition 2. The transition from low to high debt brings the investment rate from a point below the socially efficient rate to a point *above* the financial autarky rate. We can summarize these results as follows:

PROPOSITION 3: A country that accumulates an external debt choses a declining investment rate that is initially set (when the external debt is nil) below the socially efficient rate and ends (when the credit ceiling is binding) above the financial autarky rate.

8.5 Conclusion

I have shown in this chapter that a country accumulating external debt
progressively reduces its growth rate. From the viewpoint of that country,
large debt implies slow growth.

This prediction, however, should not be confused with another one,
based on a comparison of different countries. Assume for instance that a
group of different debtors are all alike except for one dimension, the cost
of debt repudiation. Once the credit ceiling binds, the larger the credit
ceiling (hence, here, the larger the country's external debt), the larger the
investment and the growth rates of the economy: indeed, when lenders
act efficiently, the service of the debt crowds *in* (rather than out) domestic
investment. The next chapter demonstrates how this conclusion might be
changed when the lenders fail to set a lending strategy that is contingent
upon the growth rate of the debtor.

Appendix A: Optimal Growth in the (Totally) Open and in the Postdefault Economy Case

The Open Economy Case

From equation (12), doubling Q_0 would also double W_0, so that one can
look for $\bar{\omega}$ such as in equation (13). $\bar{\omega}$ is the solution to the following
Bellman's equation underlying the definition of W_0 in equation (12):

$$\bar{\omega} = \underset{x}{\text{Max}} \left\{ 1 - x\left(1 + \frac{1}{2}\phi ax\right) + \frac{\bar{\omega}}{1+r}(1 + ax - d) \right\}. \tag{A.1}$$

The equilibrium value of $\bar{x}$ is

$$\bar{x} = \frac{1}{\phi a}\left[\frac{\bar{\omega}a}{1+r} - 1\right]. \tag{A.2}$$

We shall assume $\bar{\omega}$ to be positive.

Equation (A1) yields that $\bar{x}$ is a solution to

$$\frac{1}{2}x^2 - x\left[\frac{r+d}{a}\right] + \frac{1}{\phi a}(a - d - r) = 0. \tag{A.3}$$

The solution that is socially efficient is

$$\bar{x} = \left(\frac{r+d}{a}\right)\left[1 - \sqrt{1 - \frac{2}{\phi}\frac{(a-d-r)a}{(r+d)^2}}\right], \tag{A.4}$$

which exists if

$$\phi > 2(a-d-r)a/(r+d)^2, \tag{A.5}$$

a condition that we shall assume to hold in all that follows. In addition, we shall assume that $\bar{x} \geqslant d$.

The Financial Autarky Case

Let us "guess' that the solution to equation (11) can indeed be written

$$U_d(Q_0) = C_y Q_0^y. \tag{A.6}$$

Then the "guess" will prove to be the right one if

$$C_y = \underset{x}{\text{Max}} \left\{\frac{1}{\gamma}[1 - x(1 + \tfrac{1}{2}\phi ax)]^{\gamma} + \beta C_y(1 + ax - d)^{\gamma}\right\}. \tag{A.7}$$

When $\gamma = 1$ and $\beta = 1/(1+r)$, C_y is simply $\bar{C}_0$ and the investment rate x coincides with that in (A.2). Whenever $\gamma < 1$ and/or $\beta < 1/(1+r)$, one can prove (when $\bar{x} \geqslant d$) that $\bar{C}_0$ is smaller than $\bar{C}$ and that the autarkic investment rate is smaller than the socially efficient rate (see Cohen 1988 for more details).

Appendix B: The "Maximum Repayment Scheme"

Because of the linear structure of the model, one has to find b^* and x^* such that

$$V_0 = \underset{b,x}{\text{Max}} \sum_{t=0}^{\infty} b \frac{Q_t}{(1+r)^t} \equiv z^* Q_0,$$

subject to

$$\sum_{t=0}^{\infty} \beta^t u[(1 - b - y)Q_t] \geqslant U_d(Q_0).$$

(The stationarity of the problem implies that this inequality, if held at time 0, will also hold at later times.)

Call $\omega(x)$ the solution to

$$W_0 \equiv \omega(x)Q_0 \equiv \sum_0^\infty \frac{Q_t}{(1 + r)^t} = \frac{1 + r}{r - (ax - d)} Q_0 \tag{A.1}$$

when the investment rate is x. The problem at hand is therefore simply that of finding

$$z^* = \underset{b;x}{\text{Max}} \, b\omega(x) \tag{A.2}$$

subject to

$$\frac{1}{\gamma} \sum_0^\infty \beta^t (1 - b - y)^\gamma Q_t^\gamma \geq U_d(Q_0). \tag{A.3}$$

(A.3) can be written

$$\frac{1}{\gamma} \sum_0^\infty \beta^t (1 - b - y)^\gamma (1 + ax - d)^{t\gamma} \geq U_d(Q_0). \tag{A.4}$$

By duality, maximizing z^* in (A.2) subject to (A.4) amounts to finding z^*, which is a solution to

$$U_d(Q_0) = \underset{x}{\text{Max}} \, \frac{1}{\gamma} \sum_0^\infty \beta^t \left(1 - \frac{z^*}{\omega(x)} - y\right)^\gamma (1 + ax - d)^{t\gamma}, \tag{A.5}$$

in which $y = x(1 + 1/2\phi ax)$.

From the definition of $\omega(x) = [(r - (ax - d))/(1 + r)]^{-1}$ in equation (A.1), this amounts to asking the country to transfer

$$P_t = bQ_t = z^* \left[\frac{r + d - ax}{1 + r}\right] Q_t,$$

in which x is freely chosen by the country so as to maximize its utility. When $h^* = z^*/(1 + r)$ this is obviously equivalent to maximizing the country's welfare subject to $D_{t-1} \leq h^* Q_t$ as stated in equations (18) and (19) in the text.

Since

$$U_d(Q_0) = \sum_0^\infty \beta^t (1 - \lambda - y_d)^\gamma (1 + ax_d - d)^{t\gamma},$$

one can also see from (A.4) that

$$b^* < \lambda \quad \text{and} \quad x^* > x_d.$$

The investment rate x^* is larger under the optimal scheme than under default. For the same argument as in appendix A, when $\beta < 1/(1 + r)$, x^* is smaller than the socially efficient rate $\bar{x}$.

Appendix C: The Crowding In of Domestic Investment

Let us prove here that the constrained investment rate x^* is an increasing function of h^* the maximum debt-to-GDP ratio. The proof is easier to write in a continuous time setting. Let

$$\int_0^\infty e^{-\delta t} \frac{C_t^\gamma}{\gamma} dt$$

be the country's intertemporal utility function, let

$$\dot{D}_t = rD_t + C_t + I_t \left(1 + \frac{1}{2}\phi \frac{I_t}{K_t}\right) - Q_t$$

be the law of motion of debt, and let $D_t \leqslant h^* Q_t$ be the credit ceiling. When the country has reached the credit ceiling, it chooses an investment rate that is a solution to

$$x^* = \text{Arg max} \frac{1}{\gamma} \frac{[1 - h^*(r + d - ax) - x(1 + \frac{1}{2}\phi ax)]^\gamma}{\delta + \gamma d - \gamma ax}.$$

The first-order condition can be written

$$\frac{1 + \phi ax - h^* a}{1 - h^*(r + d - ax) - x(1 + \frac{1}{2}\phi ax)} = \frac{a}{\delta + \gamma d - \gamma ax}.$$

From this condition, we first learn that

$$h^* a \leqslant 1 + \phi ax.$$

We may then rewrite the first-order condition as follows:

$$[1 + \phi ax][\delta - \gamma n] = a[1 - x(1 + \frac{1}{2}\phi ax)] + a[\delta - r + (1 - \gamma)n],$$

in which $n = ax - d$.

To find the dependency of x on h^*, we differentiate both sides of the equation. We find

$$\{(\delta - \gamma n)\phi + (1 - \gamma)[1 - ah^* + \phi ax]\}\, dx = [\delta - r + (1 - \gamma)n]\, dh^*.$$

To the extent that we have shown that $h^*a \leqslant 1 + \phi ax$, one sees that $dx/dh^* > 0$. Q.E.D.

9 Large Debt and Slow Growth in the 1980s

Growth depends on capital accumulation, which in turn depends on the country's access to the world financial markets (and the rate of interest that prevails on these markets). As a heuristic tool of description of the three decades spanning from the 1960s to the 1980s, one can make the three following approximations:

1. *The 1960s* were characterized by very few private loans to LDCs. LDCs drained resources from abroad mainly as the result of public assistance. In 1970, more than half of their debt was owed to public agencies (bilateral or multilateral). Their trade balance deficit was moderate (between 2% and 3% of their GNP). The investment rate was certainly above the rate that would have prevailed at financial autarky, but presumably not very far off.

2. *The 1970s* (which we shall take as a generic term covering the period 1973–1981) can be interpreted instead as bringing renewed (and unexpected) access to the world financial markets. The trade balance deficit jumped to 7% or 8% of GDP. In terms of the transition path described in section 8.4.3 this period can be characterized as the early stage of a new borrowing process. The investment rate reached a level that initially was near the socially efficient rate (which maximizes the wealth of the nation when measured at world market prices).

3. *The 1980s* (which we take as a generic term for the period that starts in 1982) were mainly characterized by an unexpected upward shift of world interest rates. (More precisely: The rise in world interest rates started earlier, in 1979, but one may say that it was only in 1982—after the Mexican debt crisis—that it was realized that the shift was permanent). This rise in interest rates can be interpreted as a reduction of the debtor nations' wealth that brought them (unexpectedly) from the early stage of the borrowing process to its late stage, when a positive net transfer is required to stabilize their debt-to-GDP ratio.

With such an interpretation, it comes as no surprise that the investment rate dropped in the 1980s. According to the implications of the model spelled out in chapter 8, however, the investment rate should not go below the financial autarky rate, which—wherever it may be—is certainly better approximated by the rate that prevailed in the 1960s than by the rate of the 1970s. With such benchmarks the decline of investment is indeed less impressive, but not insignificant. For the highly indebted countries, investment fell from 21% of GDP in the 1960s to 19% in the late 1980s. (See table I.4 in the appendix to the introduction.)

The reader is obviously not asked to take at face value this rough description of the past three decades. What does emerge from it, however, is the fact that investment rates in the 1980s were not abnormally low when compared to those of the 1960s. They are only low when compared to the 1970s, but that rate—for all of the reasons spelled out before—is in no way an appropriate benchmark.

Casual observation of the chronicle of the rescheduling process in the 1980s casts some doubt, however, on the idea that the service of the debt generally crowded *in* domestic investment (as suggested in the model shown in chapter 8). Most economic analysts in the 1980s took the view that debt acted as a tax on the domestic economy, a tax that seems to have crowded *out* investment.

In this chapter, I indicate why such an equilibrium can occur, and I offer an empirical test of this crowding out effect. I show that it results from the inability of the lenders to commit their rescheduling strategy to being contingent upon both the investment of the country and upon an objective evaluation of the market price of the debt.

9.1   Why the Rescheduling of the Debt May Crowd Out Investment

9.1.1   Time Inconsistency of the Lenders' First-Best Policy

A key feature of the optimal rescheduling strategy described in section 8.4 is that lenders should let the debt grow along with the growth rate of the borrower's economy. As shown in chapter 8, this implies that the service of the debt is negatively correlated with the investment decision of the borrower. Even though such behavior is in the lenders' self-interest, I want to show that this is *not* a "time-consistent" decision, that is, it is an optimal decision only if the lenders can *commit* themselves (in whatever way— sophisticated contracting or a built-in reputation) to implement it later on. To see why such a commitment is necessary, assume instead that the lenders operate on a period-by-period basis and simply reschedule the debt each period to the best of their ability, taking for granted that they will do the same (and will be expected to do so) later on. Such a policy can be characterized as a "time-consistent" policy: it is one that is found to be optimal to implement today, given that it is expected to be implemented in the future. Since the work by Kydland and Prescott (1977) or Calvo (1978), it is well known that such a policy may be intertemporally suboptimal. Let us see the outcome of such a time-consistent rescheduling strategy.

As shown in Cohen and Michel 1988, calculating a time-consistent policy simply amounts to finding a feedback decision rule, which can be written

$$P_t = bQ_t, \tag{1}$$

in which b is the largest amount that the lenders can ask at time t when it is expected that *future* payments will be set according to *another* rule:

$$P_{t+s} = b^*Q_{t+s}, \tag{2}$$

which they take as given. A time-consistent strategy is one for which, at the equilibrium, $b^* = b$.

The equilibrium is calculated in appendix A. It is shown that the equilibrium growth rate is nothing but the post-default path and that $b^* = \lambda$. In other words, the time-consistent policy is one in which the lenders grasp, in every period, the costs the borrower would incur by defaulting and, as a result, their rescheduling strategy simply mimics the post-default path that the country could follow on its own.

As is apparent from equation (1), a time-consistent rescheduling strategy acts as a tax on output: the borrower expects that the lenders will ask for as much as it can pay, and this is an amount that, it can foresee, will be proportional to how much output it can generate. These expectations increase the shadow cost of capital in the debtor country and immediately reduce investment, making it optimal for the lenders to do what they are expected to: disregard the incentive to invest and ask for as much as they can.

It is this downward spiral that I think most people have in mind when disscussing the debt overhang problem: debt acts as a tax that inefficiently discourages investment, and lower annual payments from the debtor would imply more overall income to the lenders. Empirically, if this equilibrium prevails, the relationship between investment and the trade balance is as follows. Call $y_{b*} \equiv x_{b*}(1 + \frac{1}{2}\phi a x_{b*})$ the gross investment rate ($\equiv J_t/Q_t$) that the country chooses when it must pay b^*Q_t every period to its creditors. y_0 is simply the autarkic investment rate. The following relationship holds (as a first-order approximation):

$$y_{b*} = y_0 - \frac{1}{1-\gamma}b^*. \tag{3}$$

Table 9.1
Domestic counterparts of net transfers abroad

	1982	1983	1984	1985	1986	1987
I	−0.20	−0.44*	−0.52**	−0.44**	−0.48**	−0.33*
C	−0.36*	−0.09	−0.22*	−0.25*	−0.26*	−0.43*
G	−0.43**	−0.47**	−0.25*	−0.31**	−0.26**	−0.23*

Significant at the: (*) 90% degree of confidence; (**) 95% degree of confidence. Source: Cohen 1990a.

The investment rate is *below* the financial autarky rate, the discrepancy being $[1/(1 - \gamma)]b^*$. $1/(1 - \gamma)$ is nothing but the intertemporal rate of substitution of the representative agent in the country. For an industrialized country it is generally assumed to be in the neighborhood of $\frac{1}{2}$. If one trusts this value, we therefore see that investment would then fall below the financial autarky by a number amounting to half the trade surplus it has generated to service its external debt. If the trade balance surplus amounts to 2% of the country's GDP, the fall of the investment rate below the financial autarky rate amounts to 1% of GDP.

In Cohen 1990a, I have estimated an equation such as (3). (The autarkic investment rate was calculated by setting at zero the effect on investment of the access to the world financial markets in the 1970s). For the rescheduling countries, one does find a negative correlation between the service of the debt and domestic investment. For each of the six years from 1982 to 1987, the estimated coefficient is shown in table 9.1 One finds a result very similar to the prediction of equation (3), when $1/(1 - \gamma) = \frac{1}{2}$. In average, 40% the service of the external debt crowded out domestic investment. Table 9.1 also shows the other domestic counterparts of the transfer paid abroad (C is private consumption, G is government expenditures, I is the investment that was crowded out by the service of the external debt, all as a percertage of GDP). For instance, in 1982, 1% of GDP paid abroad crowded out investment by 0.2%, domestic consumption by 0.36%, and government expenditures by 0.43%. (The sum must add to one by virtue of the national account identity.)

9.1.2 Multiyear Rescheduling Agreements

Let us now assume indeed that the lenders fail to commit their policy to the constrained first best and impose an inefficient investment rate such as in (3). What should they do to improve upon the equilibrium and raise the growth rate of the debtor's economy (*and* their own return)?

In the past few years many advocates of debt relief have urged creditors to write off part of their claims to scale down the service of the debt and speed up growth in the debtors' economies (1). Let us now analyze, in the framework presented above, the rationale behind the debt relief argument.

Assume, first, that debt is *above* the credit ceiling h^*Q, which the lenders should optimally set so as to reach an efficient repayment strategy. In that case, indeed, the best thing for lenders to do is to write off the debt to h^*Q and ask the debtor to stabilize the newly written-down debt-to-GDP ratio. Note, however, that doing this will not solve the *commitment* question. The lenders must still reschedule the newly written-down debt contingent on the country's growth. If they cannot monitor investment and cannot commit their strategy to depend on past performance, writting down the debt to h^*Q_t will not in itself be sufficient to raise the efficiency of the rescheduling process. What should they then do, if they cannot reach this (constrained) first best? One simple way is to offer the country a multiyear rescheduling agreement (MYRA). This amounts to asking the country to perform an uncontingent (open-loop) payment:

$$P_t = P_0 e^{gt}, \tag{4}$$

which is not explicity contingent upon the country's performance. Such an open-loop repayment scheme avoids the negative externality of payment on growth (but obviously does not yield the crowding *in* effect of investment). When P_0 and g are calculated by the lenders so as to maximize their return and keep the country from defaulting, the country's equilibrium growth rate is simply the *financial autarky rate*. A MYRA avoids the downfall of growth and investment below the rates that are characteristic of the debt overhang such as defined in section 9.1.1. Lenders, on the other hand, must write off the debt to a value of

$$V_0 = \sum_0^\infty \frac{1}{(1+r)^t} P_t,$$

which is below h^*Q_t, the efficient ceiling.

The rationale for a write-off of the debt accompanied by a multiyear rescheduling agreement hinges on the assumption that the economy's characteristics are fully mastered by the creditors and *not* subject to exogenous shocks that would force a revision of the MYRA. In a stochastic world, lenders are less willing to grant a debt relief agreement of the variety suggested above. Perhaps a good shock will happen in the future (a gold mine is discovered) and having written down the debt will prove in retrospect to have been a fatal mistake. It is to such a case, in which the country's growth rate is subject to exogenous shocks, that I now turn.

9.2   Rescheduling (and Writing Down) the Debt in an Uncertain World

In a deterministic environment, it is perfectly useless for creditors to keep the face value of the debt above its market value. By definition, the discrepancy between the two will *not* be serviced. In a stochastic environment, instead, the lenders will certainly want to keep the face value of the debt above its market value, so as to take advantage of a sequence of a good draw that could raise the debtor's solvency above its expected average. But how should they reschedule the debt? By paying any attention to its face value, or by focusing instead only on its market value? We shall now see that the latter applies: the lenders must scale the service of the debt to its market value and totally disregard its face value.

9.2.1   A Model with Stochastic Disturbances

Consider the following version of the model examined in chapter 8. Keep all equations (1) to (6) in chapter 8 unchanged, except equation (2), the law of motion of domestic capital. Assume instead that capital is driven by the following stochastic law of motion:

$$K_{t+1} = [K_t(1 - d) + I_t][1 + \theta_{t+1}]. \tag{5}$$

θ_t is a stochastic process that takes two values u and v according to the following distribution:

$\theta_t = u$ with probability p

$\theta_t = v$ with probability $1 - p$,

with $u > v$. θ_t is an independently and identically distributed (iid) process. When $\theta_t = u$, we shall say that the economy is in a good state of nature. When $\theta_t = v$, the economy is in a *bad* state. θ_t can be interpreted as an exogenous stochastic shock upon which depends the productivity of installed capital.

Except for this modification, the rest of the economy is as in chapter 8. In exactly the same way, financial autarky or free access to the world financial markets are each characterized by a fixed investment rate x_0 and $\bar{x}$ respectively, with $x_0 < \bar{x}$ (see Cohen 1988b). Contrary to the deterministic case, the growth rate of the economy now follows a stochastic process. It is worth

$$\begin{cases} n_t = (1 + ax - d)(1 + u) & \text{when } \theta_t = u \\ n_t = (1 + ax - d)(1 + v) & \text{when } \theta_t = v, \end{cases} \tag{6}$$

when the investment rate x has been chosen at time $t - 1$ by the economy.

As in the deterministic case, one can show that the maximum repayment strategy that the lenders would want the country to implement (so as to maximize the expected present value of the country's transfers) involves a fixed investment rate x^*. Call V_t^* the maximum repayment value that the lenders would then extract. In exactly the same way as in the deterministic case, V_t^* is a linear function of current output:

$$V_t^* = z^* Q_t \tag{7}$$

V_t^* is obtained by forcing the country to invest x^* and to pay $b^* Q_t$ to the creditors, in which b^* can be written

$$b^* = z^* \{(1 + r) - [p(1 + u) + (1 - p)(1 + v)][1 + ax - d]\}, \tag{8}$$

in which z^* is the coefficient shown in equation (7).

9.2.2 How to Implement the Maximum Repayment Scheme

I will now indicate how the lenders can indeed capture the maximum repayment scheme even when they do not monitor the investment and consumption choices of the borrower and when the debt is large but finite. Consider the following decomposition of the debt:

$$D_t = V_t^* + R_t, \tag{9}$$

in which D_t is the face value of the debt, V_t^* is the maximum value calculated above, and R_t is the residual. I will asume that D_t is large enough that R_t is positive and above a threshold value calculated below. Assume that the lenders fictitiously regard R_t as a nonperforming asset and only insist on

V_t^* being serviced (while R_t is automatically capitalized). Furthermore, assume that, each period, they ask the borrower to transfer an amount P_t, which is what is necessary to keep V_t^* growing at the *expected* growth rate of the economy.

Under these assumptions P_t must solve

$$V_{t+1}^* = (1 + r)V_t^* - P_t = (1 + \theta)(1 + ax - d)V_t^*, \tag{10}$$

in which $(1 + \theta)(1 + ax - d) \equiv p(1 + u)(1 + ax - d) + (1 - p)(1 + v)(1 + ax - d)$ is the expected growth rate of the economy when the investment rate x has been selected by the debtor. P_t is then given by

$$P_t = [(1 + r) - (1 + \theta)(1 + ax - d)]V_t^*, \tag{11}$$

that is,

$$P_t = z^*[(1 + r) - (1 + \theta)(1 + ax - d)]Q_t. \tag{12}$$

For exactly the same reason as in the deterministic case, the optimum investment decision then chosen by the country will coincide with the maximum repayment strategy defined above. Provided that the nonperforming asset is initially large enough, which amounts to assuming that $D/Q \geqslant h^*$ with h^* being a given threshold, this scheme can be repeated forever and indeed deliver the maximum repayment scheme (see appendix B for further details). This shows that $V_t^* = z^*Q_t$ is simply the (ex-post) market value of the debt.

It is crucial to note that this fictitious decomposition of the debt into a performing and a nonperforming part is updated each period. Indeed, along equation (19) V^* is only left to grow at a rate $(1 + \theta)(1 + ax - d)$ that is the average growth rate of the economy. If things go well, the *actual* growth rate will be larger and V_{t+1} must be scaled up; conversely, V_{t+1} will be scaled down if growth is slow.

The second crucial remark is the following: the performing asset is not calculated from the *observation* of the market value of the debt but from the *theoretical* computation of the maximum repayment scheme. Even though they do coincide at the equilibrium, it is crucial that the lenders do not let P_t depend on the observed market value of D_t. Indeed, if they were to do so, they would ask to be repaid

$$P_t = z(x)[(1 + r) - (1 + \theta)(1 + ax - d)]Q_t,$$

and now the country would be induced to bring down the market value of the debt. These results can be summarized as follows:

PROPOSITION 2:   When the debt-to-GNP ratio is above a floor value h^*, the lenders can capture the maximum repayment value V^* by proceeding as follows. They should fictitiously split the debt into a performing and a nonperforming component, the performing component being equal to V^*. Each period, they should ask the borrower to service the performing component of the debt only and let the performing component grow at a rate equal to the expected growth rate of the economy. Meanwhile, the nonperforming asset is automatically capitalized at the riskless rate. When the actual growth rate of the economy is above (respectively below) its expected level, the performing part of the debt is scaled up (respectively scaled down). When this rescheduling strategy is undertaken, the equilibrium market value of the debt is equal to V^*.

Now, obviously, as time passes, the size of the nonperforming asset grows relative to the performing one, and some write-off of the debt may become possible without impairing the lenders' ability to capture V^*. One can actually show:

PROPOSITION 3:   When the debt-to-GDP ratio is above the threshold h^*, the debt can be written down to h^* GDP without impairing the lenders' return. If the write-off is repeated each time the economy experiences low growth and if the rescheduling is undertaken according to Proposition 2's technique, the lenders capture the maximum repayment scheme, while the market price of the debt is stabilized at a constant equilibrium price below par.

One important implication of Proposition 3 is that it is not enough to observe a discount on the debt to warrant a write-off. The intuition is that the discount on the debt takes into account the possibility that the economy may arrive at equilibrium. Lenders have no reason to write off the debt before that prediction materializes. It is only in the deterministic case when $u = v$ that the optimal strategy is indeed to write off the debt "once and for all" (to erase whatever backward shocks may have lifted the debt-to-GDP ratio above h^*) and let the debt be quoted at par.

In the stochastic case, instead, lenders want to keep a nonperforming asset in their books so as to be able to absorb a sequence of good shocks that would raise the country's solvency. The implication of this analysis is therefore that lenders are not likely to write down the debt to its market value, even though, as far as the service of the debt is concerned, they do want to act "as if" the debt were equal to its market value.

9.2.3   A Suggestion for Simplifying the Rescheduling of the Debt

Lenders, rather than fictitiously scaling *down* the outstanding debt on its market value, may as well scale *up* the value of the *flows* transferred by the debtor. To see this, assume that the borrower's transfers of resources are fictitiously priced at the equilibrium market price p_t^*, that is, assume that a transfer P_t is counted as $(1/p_t^*)P_t$. In that case, the law of motion of the debt can be written

$$D_t = (1 + r)D_{t-1} - \frac{1}{p_t^*}P_t, \tag{14}$$

that is,

$$p_t^* D_t = (1 + r)p_t^* D_{t-1} - P_t.$$

If the transfers P_t are designed to let the debt grow at the rate $(1 + \theta)(1 + ax - d)$, the payment P_t must be equivalent to the optimal rescheduling strategy. Here, instead of writing off the *stock* of the debt, only the *flows* benefit from the market discount.

One may see that actually (rather than fictitiously) implementing such a scheme is equivalent to the first best if and only if it is implemented when $p \leqslant p^*$ (defined in Proposition 3). Otherwise, the lenders may lose if a sequence of good shocks were to raise the price at par (and keep them from implementing, from then on, the optimal strategy). It is crucial to note, however, that *actually* implementing such a scheme would be much less costly to the lenders than actually writing off the debt to its market value. Indeed, only flows benefit from the market discount, not the full stock of the outstanding debt. If a sequence of good shocks occur, the equilibrium market price will go up so that the "gift" will progressively shrink as the country does better. If confronted with a credibility problem, the lenders much prefer implementing this rescheduling strategy to the strategy of writing down the stocks.

When the flows transferred by the debtor are priced at their market terms, debt rescheduling is now equivalent to that prevailing in the deterministic case: all the lenders have to do is let the debtor stabilize the debt-to-GDP ratio. The fear that "too much" is asked from the country (inefficiently crowding out investment—a fear that is the core of the debt overhang literature) now parallels the fear that the flows paid by the country are not appropriately priced (at their market term).

9.3 Conclusion

The debate on debt relief has hinged on whether too large a debt can become counterproductive, not only to the country itself but to the lenders as well. The idea of a debt overhang (exposed in Sachs 1988 and in Krugman 1988) suggests that too large a debt may impose a slowdown of growth that reduces the long-run ability of the country to service its debt to the extent that lenders, under certain circumstances, may lose from it. Can there be a debt Laffer curve problem (Krugman 1988), that is, can returns that the lenders receive on their claims go through a maximum and then *decline* as the debt rises? If a positive answer were given to this question (and if some countries were shown to have passed the point of decreasing returns), then a good case for a partial write-off of the debt could be made, a case lenders should accept.

The idea that lenders should reduce their claims in order to increase their return is a strange one to most of them. (Empirically, we have seen in chapter 4 that there were very few countries with a *negative* marginal price.) If there is a level of debt that maximizes their return, can't the lenders always act "as if" their claims were indeed equal to that level and let the difference "sleep"? Formally, we have shown in this chapter that this is exactly how lenders *should* operate. They should compute a theoretical benchmark value and act as if their claims only amounted to that value. At the equilibrium, the benchmark value on which they should scale the service of the debt is nothing but the market value of the debt itself (which, in theory, is observable on the secondary market).

If lenders act in such an efficient manner, a formal write-off of the debt is not necessary: for all practical matters, lenders act "as if" it were done, and, in addition, unexpected good luck may raise the ability of the country to service its debt, so that not explicitly writing down the debt may be rewarding.

To be effective, however, the strategy of scaling down the service of the debt on its market value needs to be *trusted*. Lack of confidence and fear of shortsighted debt management can be devastating: the debt overhang may trap the economy into slower growth than necessary. Fearing that the lenders will not reschedule their debt generously enough, the debtor may perceive a lower return to its investment in the future and immediately cut its investment, self-fulfillingly inducing the lenders to tighten their lending strategy.

I have offered an empirical estimate of the cost of such inefficiency: when it occurs, the crowding out of investment is about half the value of the transfers that are performed by the debtor. In order to get out of this downward spiral, lenders must do more than act "as if" the debt amounted to its market value. They should *actually* (rather than fictitiously) price the *flows* of transfers paid by the debtor at their market value. They should not be expected, however, to go all the way toward writing down the *stock* of debt to its market value.

Appendix A: The Crowding Out of Investment

The "time-consistent" (Nash-subgame) perfect equilibrium is one in which each player chooses the best feedback policy in response to the other player's optimal feedback policy. Here, the creditors are expected to require $P_t = b^* Q_t$ to be paid by the debtor and, in response, the debtor chooses an optimum investment decision $I_t = x^* \cdot Q_t$. One can check straightforwardly that $b^* = \lambda$ (the cost of debt repudiation) is an equilibrium strategy for the creditor. Indeed, assume that both the lenders and the debtor expect, at some time t, that the post-default path will be the equilibrium outcome of the game in future periods. Let $P_t = vQ_t$ be the payment chosen by the lenders at time t. The country chooses its investment rate to solve

$$C(v) = \left\{ \underset{x}{\text{Max}} \; \frac{1}{\gamma} [1 - x(1 + \tfrac{1}{2}\phi ax) - v]^\gamma + \beta C_d(1 + ax - d)^\gamma \right\}.$$

Because of the envelope theorem it is clear that $C(v)$ is a decreasing function of v. On the other hand, by definition of C_d, $C(\lambda) = C_d$, lenders will always find it optimal to ask that $v = \lambda$. Asking that $v > \lambda$ would induce the country to default; asking that $v < \lambda$ would be a waste of money, from the lenders' viewpoint.

If order to find the optimal response of the country when it is asked to pay $P_t = b^* Q_t$ all the time, let us use the continuous time version of the model, as spelled out in appendix 8C. The debtor's first-order condition is a solution to

$$\text{Max} \frac{1}{\gamma} [1 - b^* - x(1 + \tfrac{1}{2}\phi ax)]^{\gamma}/(\delta + \gamma d - \gamma ax).$$

It can be written

$$\frac{1 + \phi ax}{1 - b^* - y} = \frac{a}{\delta + \gamma d - \gamma x}.$$

Neglecting the adjustment cost ϕax, one finds

$$x = \frac{1 - (\delta + \gamma d)/a}{1 - \gamma} - \frac{b^*}{1 - \gamma},$$

which is the equation referred to in (3).

Appendix B: The Debt Ceiling Ratio in the Stochastic Case

To implement the maximum repayment scheme along the line of Proposition 2, an infinite nominal debt is sufficient, but not necessary. Indeed, consider the threshold

$$h^* = z^* \frac{(1 + r) - (1 + \theta)(1 + ax^* - d)}{(1 + r) - (1 + u)(1 + ax^* - d)} (> z^*),$$

and assume that the face value of the debt is initially at $D_t = h^* Q_t$. Requiring the debtor to pay $P_t = z^*[(1 + r) - (1 + \theta)(1 + ax^* - d)]Q$ implies that the face value of the debt at time $t + 1$ is

$$D_{t+1} = (1 + r)D_t - P_t$$

$$= h^*[1 + ax^* - d][1 + u]Q_t.$$

Now two things can happen. If the good state materializes, one has $Q_{t+1} = (1 + u)(1 + ax^* - d)Q_t$ so that $D_{t+1} = h^* Q_{t+1}$. If the bad state materializes, the debt-to-GDP ratio increases and debtor can write down $(u - v)(1 + ax^* - d)Q_t$ and bring the debt-to-GDP ratio back to h^*. In all instances, the lenders can indefinitely keep the debt-to-GDP ratio at level h^* while implementing the maximum repayment scheme.

10 Conclusion: From the Baker and Brady Plans Onward

10.1 Origin of the Crisis

This book has primarily interpreted the debt crisis of the 1980s as the effect of the switch in the hierarchy between growth and interest rates that prevailed in the 1970s. Had the growth rate of the debtor countries remained above world interest rates, time would have necessarily been on the debtors' side. Rescheduling the debt, holding the trade balance in mere equilibrium, would have brought the debt-to-GDP and debt-to-export ratios down and necessarily kept the countries from the temptation to default.

The 1980s was the first decade since the 1930s in which growth rates went systematically below interest rates. Because of this switch in the hierarchy between growth and interest, the burden of keeping the debt-to-export ratio from exploding became a nontrivial one.

Debtors had to stop draining resources from abroad, count on their own savings to finance their investment and, in addition, they had to transfer abroad net flows of resources to service their debt. The damage inflicted on the indebted countries by this change of regime must be carefully split into two categories. On the one hand, a debtor country had to live within its means. That meant, for the government, cut spending and/or raise taxes; for the country as a whole it meant produce at least as much as consume, and invest. The example of Brazil has shown that the latter adjustment may have taken place while the former fell (sometimes well) behind.

The second question raised by the switch of regime that occurred in the 1980s is that of assessing the efficiency of the rescheduling process. The argument against the idea that an efficient rescheduling took place can be summarized as follows. Debtors were not encouraged to make the effort of adjusting their economies because they felt that at least part of the gains arising from these efforts would be absorbed by their creditors. Debt, if inappropriately dealt with, inefficiently crowds out the investments that the country should undertake to adjust to the new economic environment.

Partly in response to such fear of an inefficient outcome, two plans have been designed by the U.S. administration: the Baker and the Brady plans, which I now briefly review.

10.2 The Baker and the Brady Plans

Each of these two plans can be rationalized with the help of the analysis spelled out in this book.

The Baker plan, in the first place, hinges on the assumption that it was feasible (in 1985) to foster simultaneously the growth and solvency of an indebted nation. This is indeed a possibility that can be rationalized using the growth model outlined in chapter 9. If it is believed that lenders act rationally only on a period-by-period basis (i.e., "time consistently"), it is indeed possible to raise the efficiency of the rescheduling process by committing (for the present *and* the future) the banking community to delivering more resources and by committing the debtor to invest these resources. As a result, *fewer* net resources are channelled to the lenders on a period-by-period basis, but *more* so on an intertemporal basis. From this analysis, the growth of the debtor appears to be a sort of intertemporal public good. More of it is beneficial to all parties, but short of a commitment that it will be supplied adequately later on, no one will supply enough of it today.

Why did the Baker plan fail (i.e., why did it need to be followed by another plan)? It is possible to argue that it failed because it put too much emphasis on the *voluntary* participation of the banking community. Indeed, if one accepts the view that growth is inefficiently dealt with because it is a public good, one can make the case that the individual and the collective rationality of lenders are two distinct notions. In that case, how can one hope to subsume the former in the latter on a "voluntary" basis? In exactly the same way as urban citizens cannot voluntarily deal with traffic jams, lenders cannot voluntarily bridge the gap between their individual viewpoints and that of the banking community as a whole. (It is crucial to note, however, that the problem faced by urban citizens is one of static coordination, whereas lenders face a dynamic problem.)

In other words, there are only two possible perspectives: it can be argued that bankers (under the auspices of their steering committee) *already* adopt a dynamically efficient viewpoint, and in that case no "plan" is needed; or one can believe that they do not attain such efficient behavior, and then no voluntary approach can be appropriate.

The Baker plan identified the insufficient supply of credit as the main cause of the debt crisis. The Brady approach postulates instead that the debt is a already too large and that it must be scaled down if any resumption of growth is to be expected. The easiest way to rationalize the Brady approach is to follow the lines of Sachs's idea of a debt overhang, or Krugman's view that there may be a debt Laffer curve problem. Just like too large a tax, too large a debt may create a disincentive to grow that may appear counterproductive to the lenders themselves.

The theoretical generality of the argument has been analyzed in chapter 9. One must wonder why is it that lenders can be trapped on the right-hand side of the Laffer curve, why they *cannot* understand that insisting on too large a payment can be counterproductive. One can answer these questions in exactly the same way as for the Baker plan: lenders as a whole may lose on an intertemporal basis, but no individual lender (nor pehaps the banking community as a whole, when they fail to commit themselves for the future) may be willing to give up its claim. Because of this dynamic coordination problem, even the lenders' steering committee may fail to narrow the gap between collective and rational behavior. If this is so, it becomes crucial to scrutinize the *new* instruments the Brady plan makes available to assess whether it can improve on the rescheduling process.

On the one hand, the Brady plan has accepted that the IMF should not make the payment of arrears a prerequisite to the signature of an adjustment program. This is certainly an important step that allows debtors to strengthen their bargaining power. On the other hand, the Brady plan called for a reopening of the "pari passu" and "negative pledge" clause, which forbids bilateral deals between debtors and creditors. Here again, one gets another way of strengthening the bargaining position of the debtors (see the bargaining model in chapter 3).

As far as debt relief is concerned, however, the only new element presented by the Brady plan consists of the possibility, open to debtors under certain conditions, of using part of the World Bank or IMF money for negotiating debt relief agreements. Taking account of the discount on the secondary markets, LDCs may hope to "buy back" their debt at an advatageous price. In a nutshell, one can view the Brady play as an attempt to replicate in a somehow systematic way the deal negotiated by Morgan Guaranty on behalf of Mexico. Yet this deal is usually regarded as a failure. The amount of debt exchanged fell short of expectations, and it is not clear how much relief the deal has brought to Mexico. In order to evaluate the Brady plan, it is therefore crucial to assess the relevance of buy-backs.

10.3 On Buy-backs

In a paper published in the *Brookings Papers on Economic Activity*, Bulow and Rogoff (1988) have usefully emphasized the difference between the marginal and the average price of the debt. The marginal price of the debt is the value for the banking community *as a whole* of one more dollar held on a debtor country. The average price, instead, is the value for one *individual* investor of one more dollar held on the country. From the econometric equations shown in chapter 4, it appears that, for most countries, the marginal price of the debt is near zero (while the average price—which, in principle, is that which is observed on the market—is 40 cents). This means that the banking community as a whole does *not* care much, on the margin, to hold one more or one less dollar on the highly indebted countries (HICs). Yet, obviously, any individual investor will wish to have more rather than fewer claims on the debtor country.

It should be noted that the discrepancy between the marginal and the average price is a feature that is also present in the case of firms. Except in the case of perfect competition *and* constant returns to scale, the marginal price of a firm's stock of capital does not necessarily coincide with its average price (see Hayashi 1982).

The reason that this is not a source of concern in the case of a firm is that a market for marginal capital can, in principle, always be created. To the extent that loans to a firm can be collateralized on the firm's capital, seniority privilege can be offered to lenders so that new (marginal) lenders are offered a property right amounting exclusively to the marginal piece of capital that they finance. In such a case, the firms are encouraged to invest up to the point where the value of the last unit they invest equals the opportunity cost of the funds they use.

In the case of a nation, no capital can be collaterized upon. Debt becomes a "public bad" and an increase in the amount due to *one* lender depreciates the value of the claim held by another. While not a cause for concern in the case of a firm, the discrepancy between the marginal and the average price of the debt becomes a source of inefficiency in the case of a nation (see chapter 4).

Let us now return to the implication of this discrepancy for the analysis of a buy-back. If a country goes on the secondary market to repurchase its debt, it will have to pay the *average* price, which is the price that an individual investor will be willing to offer. Yet, as far as the real burden of the debt is concerned, it is the *marginal* price that matters: it is the price the banking community as a *whole* attaches to the amount of debt repurchased on the secondary market. From this analysis, Bulow and Rogoff (1988) concluded that buy-backs are not likely to be a good bargain for the debtor.

10.4   How Should the Debt Be Reduced?

As pointed out by Dooley (1987), however, buy-backs are not always a bad deal. When the country makes a buy-back using reserves that would otherwise have been given (at their face value) to the lenders, the buy-back is in fact a good deal: whatever the discount, it is always better for the country to use one dollar of reserves to repurchase two dollars of debt than to use that dollar to redeem one dollar of interest.

In fact, it is possible to argue that such a scheme is exactly the efficient way (from both the country's and the lenders' viewpoint) to proceed. Indeed, to all investors in the world but one, purchasing one dollar of nominal claims on, say, Brazil costs, say, fifty cents. The one exception is Brazil itself. When Brazil repays its debt, one dollar of surplus buys one dollar of principal or one dollar of interest falling due, and not two.

To any economist raised with the idea that relative price distortions are a prima facie case of inefficiency, this discrepancy is an indication that something may be wrong. Indeed, I have argued that this relative price distortion must carefully be taken into account by lenders when they reschedule debt. It is unlikely that lenders would agree to go all the way toward writing down the debt to its face value, but there is a simpler technique to offer the debtor the same relative price as other investors.

When a debtor generates on dollar of surplus, this dollar of "hard currency" should be "counted" as two dollars, if the equilibrium average price of the debt is fifty cents on the dollar. Another manner of offering the same proposal may come as follows. If the "true" market price of Brazilian debt is fifty cents on the dollar, then any dollar of interest paid by Brazil should be accompanied by an "interest holiday" of one dollar also. (See chapter 9 for the definition of the "true" market price and a more detailed account of the underlying hypotheses supporting this scheme.) As long as one wants to enhance the collective rationality of the rescheduling process, lenders should be *compelled* (and not simply "encouraged," if one wants to avoid the "free-riding" problem) to agree with the debtor on a market price at which the *flows* of resources transferred by the debtor should be valued.

To see why such a scheme can avoid an inefficient crowding out of investment, it is enough to compare the incentives to adjust that it triggers to those that would prevail otherwise. When inappropriately rescheduled, the debt discourages the country from adusting to the extent that it may fear that part of its efforts will be siphoned off by its creditors. Now consider the following practical version of the scheme suggested above. Assume that any country that signs a stabilization program with the IMF or the World Bank is rewarded with a deal in which the debtor may use the resources that it can mobilize to repurchase its debt at a discount (agreed upon ex ante with its creditors) for, say, a period of ten years. In this case, if the discount is large enough, the country is really *encouraged* to adjust as fast as it can so as to benefit from this opportunity of repurchasing its debt at a good price. On the other hand, ten years later, the creditors can recontract the deal and raise the price at which the country can repurchase its debt, so that lenders do not necessarily have to lose too much to induce the country to adjust.

This scheme shows that it is certainly possible to encourage rather than discourage the country to adjust. It also shows why lenders must be *committed* to such a scheme: it is crucial indeed that the debtor trusts that the price at which it can repurchase its debt, agreed upon *ex ante*, will not be scaled up too soon (as early as the creditor has seen that the country has adjusted). This is why the industrialized countries, and specifically the IMF or the World Bank, are needed to make sure that the deal is trustworthy.

To summarize, the scheme that I suggest has important features that distinguish it from others. The first one is that it makes debt relief contingent upon the effort undertaken by the country. This key feature explains why it can be Pareto-improving. The second important feature—which explains why lenders should accept it—is that this "interest holiday" proposal does not lock lenders into a "once and for all" (stock) debt relief. They keep an important element of flexibility for the future and can afford to be much more generous on flows rather than on stocks. In one form or another, these are two features that any alternative plan certainly must include. Unfortunately they are both sorely missing from most of the plans offered in the 1980s.

A third important feature of the scheme is the role of a third party (the IMF, World Bank, or the industrialized countries) to monitor the deal. There are many other political and economic reasons, which this book has not reviewed, that explain why the debt of LDCs has also become a "public bad" for the *lending countries* and why they cannot simply wait for the banks and the debtors to find their own way out of the crisis. Whether the lending or borrowing side of the coin is considered, all parties should now acknowledge that sovereign debt has ceased to be a strictly private matter.

Notes

Introduction

An in-depth analysis of the debt crisis in the 1980s can be found in Sachs 1989. For an analysis of the debt crisis in the 1930s, see Eichengreen and Portes 1989. The classic earlier book on default in the 1930s is Winkler's *Foreign bonds: An Autopsy* (1933), from which the title of this book is partially borrowed. See also Sachs 1982 for a historical description that encompasses nineteenth-century episodes, and Lindert and Morton 1989.

The *World Bank Development Report* (1985) is a very useful work that encompasses early historical developments as well as a description of the debt crisis in the mid-1980s. One will also usefully read the conference volumes published by the World Bank in 1985 (Smith and Cuddington 1985) and 1989 (Husain and Diwan 1989) and see how the dominant theme has evolved from rescheduling the debt to writing it down.

Chapter 1

The intertemporal approach to economics, in its modern form, was developed by Ramsey (1928). Paying attention to the case of perfect financial markets in which agents have perfect foresight or rational expectations has led economists to discover an increasing number of "neutrality" theorems. The two most famous are perhaps the theorems of Modigliani and Miller (1958) (which states that the financial policy of a firm is irrelevant) and of Barro (which states that the financial policy of a government is irrelevant); each is stated in its crudest form in this chapter. The application of intertemporal analysis to open economies can be traced back to Bazdarich (1978), Dornbusch and Fischer (1980), Sachs (1981), and Razin and Svensson (1983), among many others. Most of the emphasis in this chapter draws on Sachs 1981. A useful approach to the intertemporal budget constraint is provided by Foley and Hellwig 1975.

Chapter 2

The overlapping generations (O.G.) model was developed by Allais (1947) and Samuelson (1958) and is the source of most counterexamples to the Barro-Ricardo irrelevance theorem. In a nutshell, it shows the relevance of the pattern of taxation across generations whenever a minimum of heterogeneity among their time horizons is considered. Blanchard (1985) and Yaari (1965) have extended the model to the case in which the lifetime of each generation is uncertain (see Blanchard and Fischer 1989 for a synthesis). Weil (1985) and Buiter (1988), relying on Blanchard's model, have shown that it is the birth of new cohorts (rather than their death) that is key to the relevance of taxation.

The analysis in this chapter draws on Sargent 1987 and Tirole 1985. See also Cass 1972 for a necessary and sufficient condition of optimality and Balasko Shell 1980 and 1981 for a rigorous mathematical exposition of the model. The papers collected in Kareken and Wallace 1980 form the best introduction to the theories that use the O.G. model for constructing a theory of money. The open economy models that use the O.G. apparatus include Buiter 1981, Dornbusch 1985, and Weil 1985. The analysis in this chapter draws on Cohen 1987b.

Chapter 3

The risk of debt repudiation has been brought to the analysis of sovereign debt by Eaton and Gersovitz's (1981a) pioneering paper. Early work on this topic also involves Kharas 1984,

Kletzer 1984, and Ozler 1986. One can read the useful survey by Eaton, Gersovita, and Stiglitz (1986) as well as the paper in the special issue of the *European Economic Review* (June 1986) for an overlook of the state of theory in 1985. An earlier useful survey is McDonald 1982. The closest parent to this analysis in the field of finance could be found (at the time these papers were written) in Jensen and Meckling 1976. See also Smith and Warner 1979. The models of debt repayment spelled out in this chapter are derived from Sachs and Cohen 1982.

More recently Bulow and Rogoff (1989a) have offered a model relying on Rubinstein's approach. Other analyses relying on Rubinstein's theory include O'Connell 1988, Eaton 1989, Fernandez and Rosenthal 1988, and Cohen and Verdier 1989.

Chapter 4

The description of the rescheduling of the debt as an attempt to made the debt contingent on the country's resources can be found in Krugman 1985 or Bulow and Rogoff 1989a. See Ozler 1986 for an empirical analysis showing that the reschedulings before 1982 could be interpreted as "new loans," while the reschedulings after 1982 should be interpreted as a partial moratorium (on this last idea, see also Kyle and Sachs 1984).

The time-inconsistency of the lending strategy of banks is closely related to the issues raised in Lucas and Stokey 1983, Persson and Svensson 1984 and Persson, Persson, and Svensson 1987. A close parent to the model presented here is Hellwig 1977. The analysis in this chapter draws on Cohen 1989 and 1991.

The discrepancy between the average and the marginal price of the debt has been recently emphasized in Bulow and Rogoff 1988. It has played an important role on the analysis of buy-backs. On that literature, see Dooley 1988, Helpman 1988, Krugman 1988, and Williamson 1988. See also Diwan and Claessens 1989 for a useful survey, and Cohen 1990b for a multiperiod approach.

1. I owe the ideas in this section to a discussion with F. Bourguignon.

Chapter 5

The analysis in this chapter draws on Cohen 1985b, 1987, and 1988c. The solvency index proposed in this chapter is nothing but the share of exports needed on average to stabilize the debt-to-export ratio. It is therefore closely related to a proposition by Bailey (1983) that debtors be asked to pay creditors a given fraction of their exports.

The idea of analyzing the law of motion of the debt-to-export ratio is key to the analysis in Cline 1983. Equation (12) is coined by Dornbusch (1989) as the Avramovic-Cline model of debt dynamics. (See Avramovic et al. 1964). Dornbusch 1989 and Dornbusch and Fischer 1985 offer insightful applications of these dynamics.

Chapter 6

The analysis in this chapter draws on Cohen 1985b. See also Cline 1983 and Feldstein 1986 for an optimistic view of the solvency of the debtors based on a similar apparatus, and Dornbusch 1989 for an ex-post reappraisal. The issue of capital flight (which is not addressed in this book) is analyzed by Cuddington (1986), who offers useful empirical estimates, and by Eaton (1987).

Chapter 7

The emphasis on the fiscal correction needed to accompany a net external transfer can be viewed as the dual question debated by Keynes and Ohlin concerning German reparations. Keynes argued that taxing the German economy was not enough to make sure that Germany would transfer *abroad* the resources needed to repay its debt obligations. The view taken in this chapter is that it is not enough to generate a trade surplus in order to repay a government's external debt. It echoes the analysis in Sargent and Wallace 1981 on the "unpleasant monetarist arithmetic." See also Buiter 1985 for an intertemporal approach to the government budget constraint that is similar to the approach employed in this chapter.

The emphasis on the fiscal dimension of the external debt is extensively addressed in Reisen and van Trotsenburg 1988 and Reisen 1989. See also Dornbusch and Simonsen 1987. The analysis in this chapter draws on Cohen 1988b and 1988c and the appendix in Cohen 1985a.

Van Wijnbergen et al. (1988) offer a very interesting application of the notions debated in this chapter to the case of Turkey.

Chapter 8

Models of endogenous growth are pioneered in Romer 1986 and 1987. Capital accumulation and external debt are analyzed in Buiter 1981 and Weil 1985 in the context of an overlapping generations model drawing on Diamond 1965. A bargaining model of debt and capital accumulation can be found in Fernandez and Rosenthal 1988 and Cohen and Verdier 1989. This chapter draws on Cohen and Sachs 1986.

Chapter 9

Besides the work by Sachs and Krugman on the debt overhang, one can also usefully read the work by Helpman (1988 and 1990) or Froot (1989). The idea that a debt write-off is needed in order to reach an efficient outcome is the core of the Brady plan offered by the U.S. administration in 1989 or by the French and the Japanese governments at the Toronto summit in 1988. The idea that the debt should be written down was put forth early on by Kenen (1983), who suggested that the industrialized countries repurchase the debt at a price below par so as to consequently write it down. See the *World Debt Tables* (1988, vol. I) and the survey in Fischer 1989 for a review of the various plans that were subsequently offered. This chapter draws on Cohen 1988b and 1990a.

Bibliography

Abel, A. (1978). "Investment and the Value of Capital," Ph.D. diss., MIT.

Allais, M. (1947). *Economie et Intérêt*. Paris: Imprimerie Nationale.

Arrow, K., and M. Kurz (1970). *Public Investment, the Rate of Return and Optimal Fiscal Policy*. Baltimore: Johns Hopkins University Press.

Avramovic, D., et al. (1964). *Economic Growth and External Debt*. Baltimore: Johns Hopkins University Press.

Bailey, N. (1983). "A Safety Net for Foreign Lending." *Business Week* 10 (January).

Balasko, Y., and K. Shell (1980). "The Overlapping Generations Model, I: The Case of Pure Exchange without Money." *Journal of Economic Theory* 23: 281–306.

Balasko, Y., and K. Shell (1981). "The Overlapping Generations Model, II: The Case of Pure Exchange with Money." *Journal of Economic Theory* 24: 112–142.

Barro, R. (1974). "Are Government Bonds Net Wealth?" *Journal of Political Economy* 82: (November): 1095–1117.

Barro, R. (1989). "Economic Growth in a Cross Section of Countries." NBER Working Paper 3120.

Bazdarich, M. (1978). "Optimal Growth and Stages in the Balance of Payments." *Journal of International Economics* 11: 425–443.

Blanchard, O. (1985). "Debt, Deficits and Finite Horizons." *Journal of Political Economy* 93: 223–247.

Blanchard, O., and S. Fischer (1989). *Lectures on Macroeconomics*. Cambridge, MA: MIT Press.

Buiter, W. (1981). "Time Preference and International Lending and Borrowing in An Overlapping Generations Model." *Journal of Political Economy* 89: 769–797.

Buiter, W. (1985). "A Guide to Public Sector Debt and Deficit." *Economic Policy* 1.

Buiter, W. (1988). "Death, Birth, Productivity Growth and Debt Neutrality." *Economic Journal* 98: 279–293.

Bulow, J., and K. Rogoff (1988). "The Buy-Back Boondoggle." *Brookings Papers on Economic Activity* 2.

Bulow, J., and K. Rogoff (1989a). "A Constant Recontracting Model of Sovereign Debt." *Journal of Political Economy* 97: 166–177.

Bulow, J., and K. Rogoff (1989b). "LDC Debt: Is to Forgive 'to Forget'," *American Economic Review*.

Calvo, G. (1978). "On the Time Consistency of Optimal Policy in a Monetary Economy," *Econometrica* 46: 1411–1428.

Cass, D. (1972). "On Capital Overaccumulation in the Aggregative, Neoclassical Model of Economic Growth: A Complete Characterization." *Journal of Economic Theory* 4: 200–223.

Claessens, S. (1988). "The Debt-Laffer Curve: Some Estimates." World Bank. Mimeo.

Cline, W. (1983). *International Debt and the Stability of the World Economy*. Washington, D.C.: Institute for International Economics.

Cohen, D. (1985a). "Inflation, Wealth and Interest Rates in an Intertemporal Optimizing Model." *Journal of Monetary Economics* (August).

Cohen, D. (1985b). "How to Evaluate the Solvency of an Indebted Nation?" *Economic Policy* 1.

Cohen, D. (1987a). "The Solvency of Indebted Nations." In Amex Awards, Winning Essays in Honor of Marjolin.

Cohen, D. (1987b). *Monnaie, Richesse et Dette des Nations.* Paris: Editions du CNRS.

Cohen, D. (1988a). "Which LDCs Are Solvent?" *European Economic Review* 32, Papers and Proceedings.

Cohen, D. (1988b). "Is the Discount on the Secondary Market a Case for LDC Debt Relief?" CEPREMAP, no. 8823.

Cohen, D. (1988c). "Domestic and External Debt Constraints of LDCs." In R. Bryant and R. Portes (eds.), *Global Macroeconomics.* London: Macmillan.

Cohen, D. (1988d). "The Management of Developing Countries' Debt: Guidelines and Application to Brazil." *World Bank Economic Review* 5.

Cohen, D. (1989). "How to Cope with a Debt Overhang: Cut Flows Rather than Stocks." In M. Husain and I. Diwan (eds.), *Dealing with the Debt Crisis.* Washington, D. C.: The World Bank.

Cohen, D. (1990a). "Slow Growth and Large LDC Debt in the 1980's: An Empirical Analysis" CEPREMAP Working Paper 9002.

Cohen, D. (1990b). "An Exact Valuation Formula for LDC Debt with an Application to the Mexican Deal." CEPREMAP Working Paper 9003.

Cohen, D. (1991). "Inefficiency of Private Credit to Sovereign States." In Paul Champseur et al., *Essays in Honor of Edmond Malinvaud* (vol. 2). Cambridge, MA: MIT Press.

Cohen, D., and P. Michel (1988). "How Should Control Theory be Used by a Time-Consistent Government?" *Review of Economic Studies* 55 (March): 263–274.

Cohen, D., and J. Sachs (1986). "Growth and External Debt under Risk of Debt Repudiation." *European Economic Review* 30 (June): 579–560.

Cohen, D., and T. Verdier (1989). "Debt, Debt Relief and Growth: A Bargaining Approach." Work Bank. Mimeo.

Cohen, D., and T. Verdier (1990). "On 'Secret' Buy-Backs." CEPREMAP. Mimeo.

Corden, M. (1988). "Debt Relief and Adjustment Incentives: A Theoretical Exploration." IMF. Mimeo.

Cuddington, J. (1986). *Capital Flight: Estimates, Issues, Explanations.* Princeton, N.J.: Princeton University, Princeton Studies in International Finance, no. 58.

Diamond, P. (1965). "National Debt in a Neoclassical Growth Model." *American Economic Review* (December).

Diwan. I., and S. Claessens (1989) "Market-based Debt Reductions." In Husain and Diwan (eds.), *Dealing with the Debt Crisis.*

Dooley, M. (1987). "Market Discounts and the Valuation of Alternative Structures for External Debt." IMF. Mimeo.

Dooley, M. (1988). "Buy Backs and the Market Valuation of External Debt. *IMF Staff Papers.*

Dornbusch, R. (1985). "Intergenerational and International Trade." *Journal of International Economics* 18 (February): 123–139.

Dornbusch, R. (1988a). "Our LDC Debts." In M. Feldstein (ed.), *The United States and the World Economy.* Chicago: University of Chicago Press.

Dornbusch, R. (1988b). *"Dollars, Debts and Deficits."* Cambridge, MA: MIT Press.

Dornbusch, R. (1989). "Debt Problems and the World Macroeconomy." In J. Sachs (ed.), *Developing Country Debt and Economic Performance*. Cambridge. MA: NBER and Chicago: University of Chicago Press.

Dornbusch, R., and M. H. Simonsen (1987). *Inflation Stabilization with Incomes Policy Support*. New York: Group of Thirty.

Dornbusch, R., and S. Fischer (1980). "Exchange Rates and the Current Account." *American Economic Review* 70: 960–971.

Dornbusch, R., and S. Fischer (1985). "The World Debt Problem: Origins and Prospects." *Journal of Development Planning* 16: 57–81.

Eaton, J. (1987). "Public Debt Guarantees and Private Capital Flight." *World Bank Economic Review* 7: 377–396.

Eaton, J. (1989). "Debt Relief and the International Enforcement of Loan Contracts." *Journal of Economic Perspectives* 4: 43–56.

Eaton, J., and M. Gersovitz (1981a) "Debt with Potential Repudiation: Theoretical and Empirical Analysis." *Review of Economic Studies* 48 (March).

Eaton, J., and M. Gersovitz (1981b). *Poor Country Borrowing in Private Financial Markets and the Repudiation Issue*. Princeton, N.J.: Princeton University Press, International Finance Section.

Edwards, S. (1986). "The Pricing of Bonds and Bank Loans." *European Economic Review* 30: 565–589.

Eichengreen, B., and R. Portes (1986). "Debt and Default in the 1930s: Causes and Consequences." *European Economic Review* 30: 599–640.

Eichengreen, B., and R. Portes (1989). "Dealing With Debt: The 1930s and the 1980s" In Husain and Diwan (eds.), *Dealing with the Debt Crisis*.

Feldstein, M. (1986). "International Debt Service and Economic Growth—Some Simple Analytics." NBER Working Paper 2046.

Fernandez, R., and R. Rosenthal (1988). "Sovereign-Debt Renegotiations: A Strategic Analysis." Boston University.

Fischer, S. (1989). "Resolving the International Debt Crisis." In Sachs (ed.), *Developing Country Debt and Economic Performance*, vol. 1.

Foley, D., and M. Hellwig (1975). "A Note on the Budget Constraint in a Model of Borrowing." *Journal of Economic Theory* 11: 305–314.

Frenkel, J., and H. Johnson (1976). *The Monetary Approach to Balance of Payments*. London: Allen and Unwin.

Frenkel, J. (1976). "A Dynamic Analysis of the Balance of Payments in a Model of Accumulation." In Frenkel and Johnson (eds.), *The Monetary Approach to the Balance of Payments*.

Froot, K. (1989) "Buy-Backs, Exit Bonds, and the Optimality of Debt and Liquidity Relief." *International Economic Review* 30 (February): 45–70.

Genotte, C., H. Kharas, and S. Sadeq (1987). "A Valuation Model for Developing-Country Debt with Endogenous Rescheduling." *World Bank Economic Review* 2 (January): 237–271.

Hayashi, F. (1982). "Tobin's Marginal q and Average q: A Neoclassical Interpretation." *Econometrica* 50 (January): 213–224.

Hellwig, M. (1977). "A Model of Borrowing and Lending with Bankrupting." *Econometrica* 49: 1879–1906.

Helpman, E. (1988). "Voluntary Debt Reduction Relief: Incentives and Welfare." IMF, Mimeo.

Helpman, E. (1990). "The Simple Analytics of Debt-Equity Swaps." *American Economic Review* 79: 440–451.

Husain, M., and I. Diwan (eds.) (1989). *Dealing with the Debt Crisis.* Washington, D.C.: The World Bank.

Jaffee, D., and F. Modigliani (1969). "A Theory of Credit Rationing." *American Economic Review* (December).

Jensen, M., and W. Meckling (1976). "Theory of the Firm: Managerial Behavior, Agency Costs and Capital Structure." *Journal of Financial Economics* 3: 305–360.

Kaletsky, A. (1985). *The Costs of Default.* A Twentieth Century Fund Paper. New York: Priority Press Publications.

Kareken, J., and N. Wallace (eds.) (1980). *Models of Monetary Economies.* Minneapolis: Federal Reserve Bank.

Kareken, J., and N. Wallace (1981). "On the Indeterminacy of Equilibrium Exchange Rates." *Quarterly Journal of Economics* 96: 207–222.

Kenen, D. (1983). *New York Times,* 6 March.

Kharas, H. (1984). "The Long-Run Creditworthiness of Developing Countries: Theory and Practice." *Quarterly Journal of Economics* 99: 415–439.

Kletzer, K. (1984). "Asymmetries of Information and LDC Borrowing with Sovereign Risk." *Economic Journal* 94: 287–307.

Krugman, P. (1985). "International Debt Strategies in an Uncertain World." In Smith and Cuddington (eds.), *International Debt and the Developing Countries.* Washington, D.C.: The World Bank.

Krugman, P. (1988). "Financing vs. Forgiving a Debt Overhang: Some Analytical Notes." *Journal of Development Economics* 29 (December): 253–268.

Kydland, F., and E. Prescott (1977). "Rules Rather than Discretion: The Inconsistency of Optimal Plans." *Journal of Political Economy* 85: 473–491.

Kyle, S., and J. Sachs (1984). "Developing Country Debt and the Market Value of Large Commercial Banks." NBER Working Paper 470.

Lindert, P., and P. Morton (1989). "How Sovereign Debt has Worked." In J. Sachs (ed.), *Developing Country Debt and Economic Performance.* Chicago: University of Chicago Press.

Lucas, R., and N. Stokey (1983). "Optimal Fiscal and Monetary Policy in an Economy without Capital." *Journal of Monetary Economics* 12: 55–94.

McDonald, C. (1982). "Debt Capacity and Developing Country Borrowing: A Survey of the Literature." *IMF Staff Papers* 29: 603–646.

Michel, P. (1982). "On the Transversality Condition in Infinite Horizon Optimal Models." *Econometrica* (July): 975–986.

Modigliani, F., and M. Miller (1958). "The Cost of Capital, Corporate Finance, and the Theory of Investment." *American Economic Review* 48: 261–297.

Nash, J. (1950). "The Bargaining Problem." *Econometrica* 28: 155–162.

Ozler, S. (1986). "The Motives for International Bank Rescheduling, 1978–1983: Theory and Evidence." UCLA, Working Paper 401; *American Economic Review.*

O'Connell, S. (1988). "A Bargaining Theory of International Reserves." University of Pennsylvania. Mimeo.

Persson, T., and L. Svensson (1984). "Time-Consistent Fiscal Policy and Government Cash Flows." *Journal of Monetary Economics* 14: 365–374.

Persson, M., T. Persson, and L. Svensson (1987). "Time Consistency of Fiscal and Monetary Policy." *Econometrica* (November).

Portes, R. (1987). "Debt and the Market." Center for Economic Policy Research. Mimeo.

Purcell, J., and D. Orlanski (1988). "Developing Countries' Loans: A New Valuation Model for Secondary Market Trading." Corporate Bond Research, Solomon Brothers Inc., June.

Ramsey (1928). "A Mathematical Theory of Saving." *Economic Journal* 38: 543–559.

Razin, A., and L. Svensson (1983). "The Terms of Trade and the Current Account: The Harberger-Laursen-Meltzer Effect." *Journal of Political Economy* 91: 97–125.

Reisen, H. (1989). "Public Debt, North and South." In Husain and Diwan (eds.), *Dealing with the Debt Crisis.*

Reisen, H., and A. Van Trotsenburg (1988). *Developing Country Debt: The Budgetary and Transfer Problem.* Paris: OECD.

Romer, P. (1986). "Increasing Returns and Long-Run Growth." *Journal of Political Economy* 94: 1002–1037.

Romer, P. (1987). "Crazy Explanations for the Productivity Slowdown." In S. Fischer (ed.), *NBER Macroeconomics Annual.* Cambridge, MA: MIT Press.

Roth, A. (1979). *Axiomatic Models of Bargaining,* Lecture Notes in Economics and Mathematical Systems, no. 170. Berlin: Springer-Verlag.

Rubinstein, A. (1982). "Perfect Equilibrium in a Bargaining Model." *Econometrica* 50: 97–109.

Sachs, J. (1981). "The Current Account and Macroeconomic Adjustment in the 1970s." *Brookings Papers on Economic Activity* 2.

Sachs, J. (1982). "LDC Debt: Problems and Prospects." In P. Wachtel (ed.), *Crises in the Economic and Financial Structure.* Lexington, MA: Lexington Books.

Sachs, J. (1984). "Theoretical Issues in International Borrowing." *Princeton Studies in International Finance* 54.

Sachs, J. (1988). "The Debt Overhang of Developing Countries." In J. de Macedo and R. Findlay (eds.), *Debt, Growth and Stabilization: Essays in Memory of Carlos Dias Alejandro.* Oxford: Blackwell.

Sachs, J. (ed.) (1989). *Developing Country Debt and Macroeconomic Performance,* vols. 1-3. Cambridge, MA: NBER, and Chicago: University of Chicago Press.

Sachs, J., and D. Cohen (1982). "LDC Debt with Default Risk." NBER Working Paper 925.

Sachs, J., and D. Cohen (1985). "LDC Borrowing with Default Risk." *Kredit und Kapital* (special issue on international banking) 8: 211–235.

Sachs, J., and H. Huizinga (1987) "US Commercial Banks and the Developing-Country Debt Crisis." *Brooking Papers on Economic Activity* 2.

Samuelson, P. A. (1958). "An Exact Consumption-Loan Model of Interest with or without the Social Contrivance of Money." *Journal of Political Economy* 68 (December): 467–487.

Sargent, T. (1979). *Macroeconomic Theory.* New York: Academic Press.

Sargent, T. (1987). *Dynamic Macroeconomic Theory.* Cambridge, MA: Harvard University Press.

Sargent, T., and N. Wallace (1981). "Some Unpleasant Monetarist Arithmetics." Federal Reserve Bank of Minneapolis, *Quarterly Review,* (October) 1–17.

Smith, G. W., and J. Cuddington (eds.) (1985). *International Debt and the Developing Countries.* Washington, D.C.: The World Bank.

Smith, C., and J. Warner (1979). "On Financial Contracting: An Analysis of Bond Covenants." *Journal of Financial Economics* 7: 117–161.

Stiglitz, J., and A. Weiss (1981). "Credit Rationing in Markets with Imperfect Information: I." *American Economic Review* 71: 393–410.

Tirole, J. (1982). "On the Possibility of Speculation Under Rational Expectations." *Econometrica* 50: 1163–1181.

Tirole, J. (1985). "Asset Bubbles and Overlapping Generations." *Econometrica* 56: 1499–1528.

van Wijnbergen, R. Anaud, and R. Rocha (1988). "Inflation, External Debt and Financial Sector Reform: A Quantitative Approach to Consistent Fiscal Policy." NBER Working Paper 2170.

Weil, P. (1985). "Essays On the Valuation of Unbacked Assets." Ph.D. diss., Harvard University.

Williamson, J. (ed.) (1985). *IMF Conditionality.* Washington, D.C.: Institute for International Economics.

Williamson, J. (1988). "Voluntary Approach to Debt Relief." Washington, D.C.: Institute for International Economics.

Winkler, M. (1933). *Foreign Bonds: An Autopsy.* Reprinted New York: Arno Press, 1976.

World Debt Tables (various editions). Washington, D.C.: The World Bank.

World Development Report (various editions.) New York: Oxford University Press for the World Bank.

Yaari, M. (1965). "Uncertain Lifetime, Life Insurance and the Theory of the Consumer." *Review of Economic Studies* (April): 137–150.

Index